Breaking Free

A Memoir

Sara Colvin

ISBN 978-1-64569-080-1 (paperback)
ISBN 978-1-64569-081-8 (digital)

Christian Faith Publishing, Inc.
832 Park Avenue
Meadville, PA 16335
www.christianfaithpublishing.com

Printed in the United States of America

ENDORSEMENTS

Sara Colvin's brutally honest *Breaking Free* is a compelling and intimate memoir focusing on one young woman's troubled early life involving the use and abuse of drugs and alcohol. Sara's life choices during her teens and early twenties ultimately lead her down a path of personal destruction onto the virtual brink of its ever-present precipice. However, through this seemingly unending addiction-ladled journey of darkness and despair, Sara awakes one day and is determined to finally find her true self. She does this through her own newly discovered inner strengths, some trusted friends, skilled and caring professionals, and most of all, God. She thus begins the slow, upward spiral to her living the full life of friend, daughter, and, most importantly, mother.

This book is a must-read to anyone suffering from addiction issues and/or helping someone else who may be addicted. Getting clean and sober *are* an absolute possibility, and Ms. Colvin tells the reader through her own moving story how at least one person managed to accomplish it. It may not be easy, but it *can* be done, and Sara shows us the way in her up-close-and-personal tale of redemption.

—James R. Fitzgerald, MS
Supervisory Special Agent, FBI (Ret.)
Profiler, Forensic Linguist
Author, *A Journey to the Center of the Mind: Books I, II, III*

As the opioid epidemic rages on, *Breaking Free…* is a timely and very important book. Ms. Colvin provides to the professional, the lay person, and those struggling in addiction a thorough, comprehensive understanding of the devastating effects of addiction and the difficulties of obtaining and maintaining recovery. She delineates some of the causes, progression, and the process of healing. The book is an inspiration to her and everyone struggling with addiction. I have over forty-five years working in the substance abuse field and can honestly state: This is one of the most cogent, pithy works on the subject that I have ever read.

—Bruce Schaffer, M.Ed., C.C.J.P.

This book is must-read for anyone who has ever loved an addict or loved someone whose life was torn apart by another person's addiction. In her brutally honest, heart-rending account of the rollercoaster life of an addict, Sara Colvin proves that addiction is a devastating illness that very few non-addicts truly understand. Reading about Sara's journey will open your eyes to unimaginable suffering and determination. Much of the book is not easy to read, but you will hopefully be a more compassionate person after you have processed Sara's painful story.

—Marsha Konell,
A mother who lost her twenty-nine-
year-old daughter to drug addiction
and is currently raising the child she left behind

I could not compile a memoir without honoring the men who personally placed me on the path of recovery. Therefore, this book is dedicated to the task force team of the Bensalem Police Department, whose combined efforts provided the catalyzing force which ended a devastating active addiction and reopened the gateway to freedom. The results of your commitment and service have proven worthwhile in the rebuilding of the foundation of my life. Without your intervention, my name would be engraved upon a tombstone, not inscribed upon a book cover. The duty of law enforcers was accomplished on that Thursday night when the team of detectives took me off the streets. Throughout the interrogation process, your sincerity and compassionate understanding amazed me. You rightfully earned the utmost respect from me and my family through your support and integrity during the trial. The unnecessary and unexpected acts of kindness by thoughtful detectives instilled within me an unceasing gratitude. Pardon my bias if I hold the Bensalem Police Department in high regard. The team rescued a lost, hopeless life from the ravages of death. You returned a daughter to her mother and gave a mother back to her daughter. Countless lives are peaceful again, because of you.

ACKNOWLEDGMENTS

God: Clearly, this is for you, by you, and through you. I continue to be rendered speechless as to Your unspeakable mercy. My life is my gift to you; my heart is Yours alone. You came through deplorable conditions—because You wanted me. You called and I continuously refused to listen. Until You picked me up out of the gutters of hell and saved me. Through the darkness, I was found. You are remarkable.

Mom: Our daily call did not merely "carry me through" as I so frequently attest. It rebuilt my soul. This book is for you because you told me I could. When one has a best friend, a mentor, a role model, a spiritual partner, a loyal companion, and a faithful confidant they are blessed to be surrounded by amazing people. But to have those very characteristics embodied in a single person is an extraordinary miracle. You are that gift to me. I would give my life for you; for you have already given so much of yours to me. I deeply admire you as my mother.

Laila: You are my angel. In your eyes I see heaven's reflection. You provide the motivation and inspiration for everything I strive to be. We've travelled this road of recovery in the past and together we'll do it again. My little co-creator, your resilience astounds me and your compassion puts me to shame. You know this book because more than anyone else, you were there with me. How many times can one child save a parent's life? You have a special purpose. Girlfriend, the best is yet to come.

My relatives—siblings, aunts and uncles, cousins, friends, and family: Your consistent and thoughtful support encouraged me through the deep loneliness of incarceration. Your acceptance strengthened me during a time of tremendous humiliation and remorse. I clung to each letter, savoring every word of each card. Thank you for showing up for me when even society had kicked me out. Grandmom knew how to hold a family together—the continual stream of mail that appeared under my cell door demonstrated that as a family, we have clearly inherited her unconditional ability to love.

Dad: Your Wednesday afternoon visits were so important to me. You always knew how to make me laugh. I enjoyed the normalcy of our conversations and the updates on *Two and a Half Men*. You were never afraid to tell me how bad I've messed up because you think it could never be worse than you. Dad, I think I've got you beat on this one. Thanks for being a father when I really needed my dad.

CONTENTS

PROLOGUE

To give a detailed account of my personal history with addiction, recovery, and relapse with two primary intentions:

     a)   To educate the professional community involved in the field of alcohol and chemical dependency

     b)   To inspire those afflicted with the disease of alcoholism and addiction

INTRODUCTION

*I*t is my experience that most people of normal, everyday functioning have a basic knowledge of addiction or at least a point of recognition with the term. Typically, everyone can think of a person battling some degree of a problem with an addictive substance or behavior. Actual understanding of the disease of addiction is less common in mainstream society. In depth comprehension is basically nonexistent outside of personal experience. However, even more unfamiliar is the process of recovery. It is my hope that this book will raise the awareness of both the addiction and addicted communities.

I wrote the first draft of this memoir while residing in the county jail—facing over a dozen serious felony charges and looking at the very real possibility of spending many years of my life as an inmate in a state prison. It was in these dire circumstances that my core belief system changed, dramatically altering the way I perceived and interacted with the world.

I had always held the underlying assumption that "as you give to the world, so the world gives to you." Through incarceration, a magnificent spiritual transformation, and focused attention my karmic operating principle was shattered and destroyed. As unsettling as this may seem, I came to realize two profound truths, namely Grace and Mercy, which provide the basis for my renewed worldview. This is beautifully articulated by Saint Paul in Romans 8:28, "We know that God causes everything to work for the good of those who love God and are called according to His purpose for them" (New Believer's Bible, NLT, 2006)

This revelatory statement crumbled my previous, erroneous mentality of "getting what you give." Granted, my old view was not entirely without beneficial impact on myself and those around me. Core beliefs filter the lens through which we view the world and in this sense, they are a contributing force in behavior. For most of my life, I had tried to be polite and courteous, wanting others to do likewise. I treated others kindly and with respect, expecting a reciprocal response. What I believed to be true about the world appeared to be working effectively. I was getting back what I was giving out.

Then I relapsed into an uncontrollable addiction. Sitting in a lonely, cold cell after surviving eighteen months of brutal, vicious powerlessness, I no longer wanted the world to give to me as I had been giving to it. In fact, getting back what I had been giving to life terrified me. If I continued to believe in a reap-what-you-sow formula for the universe, I was in big trouble. Looking at the extent of the damage I had caused throughout a devastating relapse, what I deserved was to be put away, miserable for a very long time.

This is precisely the point where I discovered the two key concepts, Grace and Mercy, which came to form the foundation for my improved ideology. These spiritual principles became more than fanciful ideals taught at Sunday school. They became spiritual realities; motivating forces guiding my life.

> Grace: getting what I do not deserve; unmerited gifts; unwarranted kindness, unjustified generosity
> Mercy: not getting what I deserve; pardoning of a wrong, forgiveness of injustice, gentle discipline

Awaiting trial, my time in jail unfolded and I watched in awe and amazement as the miracles of Grace and Mercy turned into tangible factual experience. One evening early on, I heard a voice clearly speaking to me, "Prepare your heart to receive my gift." I cannot adequately explain in scientific terms how I recognized the voice of God. Perhaps the best description I can offer is that of nostalgic familiarity. I immediately and intuitively knew I was being directed onto a journey to be illuminated by revelation and marked by agony and ecstasy.

Alone and secluded in the darkness of confinement, I committed to embark upon the path ahead.

I could not say at the time that I was grateful for the experience of being incarcerated or for the total destruction created through relapse. I can now acknowledge numerous gifts received during that period of seclusion such as spiritual purification, renewed purpose and direction, emotional maturity, and God-awareness. There was definite profound growth, intense insights, and life-altering shifts of perception. However, I simply cannot justify personal spiritual awareness at the cost of the massive upheaval that occurred in my young daughter's life as a result of my poor choices. I admit that God made the best out of a bad situation and I was led to find the diamond in the mud. Far from glorifying incarceration to any extent, I vigorously hold to the opinion that there could have been another way. At many points throughout my downfall, I could have chosen differently.

After nine and a half years of recovery, I had built a successful life for myself and Laila, my only child. A life we both found to be rewarding, exciting, and prosperous. Then I relapsed into an uncontrollable addiction which ultimately ended in the back of a police car, hands and feet bound by shackles and handcuffs. While actively drinking and drugging, I lost, sold, stole, or gave away everything we once had and entirely uprooted the life of an eleven-year-old girl. Laila had grown up in a recovery environment and understood what active addiction can do to lives but it wasn't personal experience for her until I returned to my former behaviors. Knowing that Laila first handedly witnessed the horrendous destruction of active addiction convinces me there could have been another way. No child should ever be exposed to the horrors detailed in this book or subjected to the neglectful abandonment characteristic of addiction. Especially not a child accustomed to a better way of life.

I will honestly state that in order for me to get sober, I had to be forced into a guarded institution with no option to leave. I will not state that I had to initially relapse or that I had to come to jail to learn invaluable life lessons or fulfill a divine plan. I had many, many choices along the way and I will not trivialize my daughter's loss. With that serving as my responsibility disclaimer, I offer this book to you—my part in making an awful situation useful to myself and others. Writing was a challenge and a blessing. Some sections flowed with great ease while with others I struggled to no satisfaction. I found that while writing, my emotions were influenced by the content. Describing the cruise ship filled me with joy and delight, whereas the trip to Costa Rica spurred deep regret. Recalling the "borderline experience" overwhelmed me with anxiety so tremendous my hands shook and I broke out in a sweat. The process of composing a memoir had its peaks and valleys with the overall task blanketed with insight and reflection. Considered by me to be one of my top personal life accomplishments (Laila holding the number one position), I send out this book with love. My intention to educate and inspire remained firm. Addiction is deadly, progressive, and incurable. There is a solution. It's called recovery and is available— and possible—for even the lifeless among the hopeless.

PART I

A New Life

Becoming Addicted

The first time I consumed alcohol, I became intoxicated to the point of stumbling home, making my way upstairs and into bed with the assistance of a friend, also a virgin drinker. I remember a wastebasket being placed near the edge of my bed, which proved a blessing numerous times over throughout that night marked by vomiting and fitful sleep. If there were any pleasant memories surrounding that evening, those details are lost in a drunken blur.

Weeks prior, I had suffered the heartbreaking pangs of losing my first love, a boyfriend I had been dating since I was twelve years old. I was now fifteen, in the ninth grade, and looking for an escape from the painful feelings of loss, depression, and confusion. Through a random occurrence, I had been told about a party happening in the woods with a group of neighborhood kids, none of which I had ever met. Every facet of this situation was a new experience for me. First, I had never before been invited to participate in anything like this. The parties I attended up to this point were preplanned occasions—with invitations sent ahead of time and balloons identifying the location so I knew where to arrive with my wrapped gift. There were also family get-togethers celebrating holidays, weddings, and the standard family events. I was raised with an exceptionally large extended family—my mother being the youngest of ten children. Spending time with my relatives was familiar to me. So far as parties were concerned, my only experience consisted of family occasions and birthday gatherings with my school friends.

I attended Catholic school for twelve years, being fully educated in the parochial school system. This entirely secluded me from the neighborhood kids attending public school. I was never cognizant of this separation until I found out other kids lived in my town and I did not know who they were. I had minimal involvement with anyone outside of classmates except during softball season. I played for the community league for eight years and although I was well liked, it was clear to me and my sister that these girls were all good friends. During softball season, I discovered that there were a lot of kids my age—residing in my own town—that were living a different life than me and my family. Boys would come to our games and practices to watch their girlfriends play or simply hang out around the field. They rode bikes even when it was dark and I never saw their parents around. This uninhibited freedom was foreign to me. Being on the softball team year after year exposed me to another way of life as I watched girls and boys in my age group have independence and privileges I had never known. They used curse words and knew the names of streets on the other side of town. I could recite every Catholic prayer and knew how to get to my grandmother's house and church. These kids kissed and wore baggy clothes. I went camping with my Girl Scout troop and dressed identical to my best friend, on purpose. We may have lived in the same community, but we were not living similar lifestyles.

I quit playing softball when I was thirteen. It was a monumental year for me, colored with drastic changes. My parent's marriage ended in divorce and my father moved out. I didn't see him again for eight years. I was about to enter high school after being in the same class, in the same building, with my same friends since kindergarten. I was full swing into puberty and had gained fifteen pounds in the eighth grade. Bras and tampons were now necessary. Most importantly, I found myself in a serious romantic relationship with a boy from school. During this tumultuous period, I clung to him for safety, comfort, and love. Through the intensity of early adolescence, I found my boyfriend to be the single stabilizing influence holding me together. I came to depend upon the relationship for everything, developing no outside friendships or support. My world shrank to include only him. During the precious formation of my young identity, I connected myself only with a boy.

When he ended our relationship, I was destroyed. Relying fully on him to a codependent degree, his breaking off our commitment shattered my poorly built sense of self. I was lost, hopeless, and depressed without him, unsure of how to cope with or manage life on my own. It was in this mind-set of despair that I agreed to attend the keg party in the woods. Any friends were better than none at all. I remembered the lack of supervision I had noticed with the kids during softball season. Here were the same boys that used to ride their bikes to the ballpark. Except now they had beer and cigarettes.

Years before, when first exposed to the neighborhood kids, curiosity sparked my interest because they lived such a different life than me. Now, when offered the opportunity to socially interact with them, curiosity struck again and I accepted. Off into the woods I went.

I don't know what brand of alcohol I drank or how much I consumed. The only person I knew was my friend from school, who was the actual recipient of the invitation. I was included simply because I was over my friend's house when they invited her. I don't think anyone there had ever seen me before or even knew my name. I am certain no one asked. The situation was uncomfortable and inappropriate for teenagers. Even in my desperate longing to fit in with the crowd, I knew I didn't belong there.

Instead of leaving and walking back to the protection of my home and the loving care of my family, I accepted the beer that was being placed into my hand and sat down on a log in front of the bonfire. I hated drinking. I saw what alcohol did. I knew the way it destroyed people, took away good lives, and ruined happy families. I had long ago sworn off any type of drinking or smoking. Those were the downfalls of my father and I was never going to be like him. Now there was a beer in my hand and a decision to be made. Peer pressure wouldn't let me stay and not drink. Fear of judgment wouldn't let me walk away alone. Emotional pain had me yearning for acceptance. I put the alcohol to my lips and drank.

I must have passed out or blacked out at some point during the night because I remember becoming aware of some guy who was trying to take advantage of my drunken state. As I attempted to push him away from me, I realized I had little muscle control. I couldn't get my arms or hands to go where I needed them to go. Without the ability to physically move properly, I felt scared and drunk.

Eventually, I returned home. My friend stayed overnight at my house and helped me crawl up the stairs to my bedroom, where she kindly planted a trashcan at the edge of my bed. Often awakening from restless slumber, I was violently ill throughout the night. In the morning, when my mother woke us up to prepare for Sunday church, I had a throbbing headache and felt weak and nauseous. As I had in early childhood, I reaffirmed my commitment to avoid drinking.

That morning happened to fall on the first day of a new month, which was significant for me because for the last few years, I had developed a habit of weighing myself on the first of every month. I was unhappy with the weight I gained in puberty and was borderline obsessive with body image, food, and weight. I recorded my weight monthly and kept track of the number in a personal weight log. I also listed the details of every food item I ate each day. This "Food Journal," as I titled it, was secretly hidden under my bed, away from prying eyes. I had the sense that this behavior was not typical of a healthy fifteen-year-old girl. Or maybe I was aware that I was cross-ing an invisible line into eating disorder territory and I didn't want anyone to find out.

That particular morning the scale read 117.5 pounds, down six pounds from last month. I was thrilled! I knew logically that the continuous puking of the previous night largely caused this sudden weight loss. I did not care that this consequence resulted from pour-ing poisonous liquid down my throat the evening before. A connec-tion had been made: throwing up leads to weight loss. I remained adamant in my refusal to drink even if it did produce an end result

I wanted. I conjured up another idea to achieve the same result: bulimia.

I kept my promise and did not pick up alcohol again but I continued to associate with the kids from the bonfire in the woods. It was through this circle of friends that I was introduced to cocaine. When it was first presented to me, I remembered the night I crushed up Ritalin pills with a girl from school and we snorted them in her bedroom on a weekend sleepover. It was shortly after my boyfriend had ended our relationship and I was feeling suicidal and apathetic. My friend had taken a few pills from her prescription bottle, crushed them into powder with a spoon, and formed two lines with an ID card. Then she rolled up a dollar bill, put it to her nose, and inhaled the Ritalin powder. When she handed the bill to me, I followed suit. The effect was exhilarating. We talked endlessly through the night, my depression lifted entirely, and I felt a renewed sense of hope and purpose. This elevated state of happiness was followed by a sharp decline in mood. As the medication started to leave my body before my brain had begun to produce the proper chemical balance, I experienced intense uncomfortableness and irritation. Being the first time I had ever felt such an ecstatic high, followed by an equally painful low, I researched Ritalin. I learned that this was the common aftereffect of stimulant drugs: a "come down" period where the body readjusts to normal functioning. I had artificially introduced chemicals into my brain which it had been accustomed to producing for itself. The brain is ingeniously responsive in that it immediately recognized that something else was doing its job and with no need for double work, stopped producing the targeted chemicals. However, there is some lag time as the brain waits to see if the chemical will again be artificially ingested, hence the feeling of discomfort. After a period of time, if an outside substance is not detected, the brain will resume its original job and once again produce the appropriate chemical balance for brain functioning.

My problem has always been one of impatience. Immediate self-indulgence remains a continuous barrier to growth. I never wanted to wait for that period of discomfort to pass and allow the brain to normalize itself. I sought the quick fix and instantaneous relief. When cocaine first became available to me, I associated the drug with the Ritalin pills my friend and I had smashed and snorted. The overwhelming depression that consumed me day and night had broken me to the point of becoming agreeable to experimentation with stimulants. The first time cocaine entered my nose I fell in love. Literally, I knew I had found the answer. Everything I had ever lacked internally was now filled to abundance. The painful sadness was not only gone but replaced with an intense exuberance. The mundaneness of everyday existence was now delightful down to the minutest detail. The agonizing boredom which plagued my soul was the most tremendous burden of all. Yet with a single line of white powder, this hindrance was miraculously transformed into active involvement with others. I could accomplish—with enthusiasm—an extensive plethora of tasks. In cocaine, I discovered what I had always been looking for in life: fulfillment, joy, and interest. Life was no longer unbearable. With cocaine, I was the girl I always knew I had inside of me.

Since cocaine fulfilled my every need, desire, and dream, I dedicated myself to it. Using cocaine became my sole purpose for living. Using cocaine became my only reason to live. I directed all my thoughts toward getting enough of the drug so that I could stay highly functional at all times. I devoted all my time to finding, planning, and scheming ways to get more of the drug. I eliminated anything from my life that distracted my attention from my new lover. I had nothing left for anything or anyone that did not aid in my pursuit for cocaine.

That included school. I dropped out at fifteen, and my mother had me put on homebound status so that I did not get charged with truancy. I attended the local Catholic school and the administration was compassionate and cooperative with my mother's requests. With the assistance of my sister, the teachers would send my assignments home.

Family no longer mattered unless I was manipulating them. I was mean and obnoxious when I did not have cocaine available. I began picking up on the behaviors of the people I was hanging around—smoking cigarettes, sneaking out of the house, stealing, running the streets, partying with older guys, making trips to the city daily, and sleeping with strangers. To my younger siblings, I had become a thoughtless and inconsiderate sister who was chaotic and scary, bringing stress and torment to their childhoods. To my mother, I was violent and offensive, causing great fear and worry to build in her heart. None of this mattered to me because cocaine was my solution and I was not giving it up. There was nothing of greater importance to me than staying loaded.

I never had any interest in using only on weekends or even part time. Cocaine was all I wanted to do, every day of the week, all day long. That is some of the reason for the rapid progression of addiction in my life. I did not start out smoking weed for five or ten years and then slowly move onto harder drugs. I did not get drunk on weekends at high school parties and develop alcoholism thirty years down the road. When I put that drug into me the first time, I signed my life over to it. The consequences of using increased quickly as I wasted no time procrastinating in my addiction. Before my sixteenth birthday, I knew I was out of control and addicted.

Less than a year into actively using cocaine, fully involved with a group of heavy drug abusers, I was brutally attacked and beaten by a neighborhood girl. It happened at a house party where earlier that night a guy had taken me into the bathroom and laid out a line on the sink for me to snort. It was darker in color and thinner in texture than what I was used to so I asked what it was. He told me it was cocaine from a new dealer and that is why it looked different. I didn't realize until years later that I had snorted my first line of heroin. I am still unaware of entirely what happened to me after I walked out of that bathroom but I am clear that I was knocked unconscious immediately from the effects of the heroin.

I returned to awareness on the floor of a living room with a fist pounding into my skull repeatedly. I think back to that night and must state that that girl probably saved my life. She may have quite literally beaten me into consciousness and out of an overdose. With my weakened strength, I haphazardly tried to shield my face but it was useless. I saw people everywhere yet no one was helping or stopping the attack. I could hear bystanders cheering this girl on as she smashed my eye sockets with her ringed knuckles. When it was over, she left. I tried to stand but my knees buckled and I could not steady myself enough to walk. As I stumbled down the hallway, someone made a comment about the trail of blood I was leaving on the carpet. Another girl screamed out, "Don't touch her. She has AIDS!" I knew I did not have the disease, but the level of humiliation I felt at that moment was incomprehensible. In complete demoralization, on my hands and knees, I crawled out the door into the blackness of the dead of night.

My mother lived three blocks from this house party. As I ventured out alone, not knowing if I was going to be followed left me shaking in terror. Covered in blood and barely coherent, I opted to take the back roads instead of the main street. I didn't know where the wounds were but I could feel my cheekbones throbbing and liquid running off my chin and swishing in my ears. I couldn't walk or see straight.

When I turned the corner onto my mother's street, a neighbor saw me and came rushing out. I was sobbing tears and dripping blood and I desperately needed a hug. I cried out his name for help. His reaction pierced the core of me. He instinctively stepped away, too horrified to touch me or come close. He ran ahead of me, silent and fast. I knew he was going to get my mom. I knew she would reach out and love me. In a condition only a mother could embrace, my mom took me into her arms and held me. The first but not the last time she would be the only person in the world who would hold my hand while I knocked on death's door.

The emergency room physicians sewed up the gashes and cleaned out the cuts. The bruises and swelling would heal in time, and I would be left with a two-inch scar under my right eye. The police detectives later told me she had worn a studded ring which caused most of the permanent damage. I received an apology letter from her a few months later, a stipulation of her probation. The beating was meant to serve as a warning to stay away from her brother, whom I was using cocaine with at the time. This is the caliber of people I associated with while using drug: violent, vengeful, feared lunatics known for raging assaults.

A few weeks later, saving grace entered my life when I found out I was pregnant. Still absolutely stunned that so many of my peers had witnessed and even encouraged the attack, this news was the deciding factor I needed to remove myself from that crowd. It could not have come at a better time—I wanted a way out. I knew I had to get away from that life and those people. I did not fit in and they did not want me around. They were more than just bad news. That circle of kids was inhumane, corrupt, and immoral on levels I was not comfortable with even on drugs. In the short time span of knowing these people, I had become unrecognizable even to myself, a monster living only for addiction, tormenting the lives of those close to me.

Pregnancy was now the reason to cut all ties. I could not change for myself but was willing to do it for the life of my unborn baby. I quit everything, instantly. I gave up smoking cigarettes, stopped taking all drugs, and refrained from sex. I enrolled back in school full-time and began college preparations. I passed my driving test and received my license. I returned to church on Sundays and participated again in family activities. My mother became my closest friend during my pregnancy. At first she was naturally upset that her sixteen-year-old daughter was going to be a mother. Soon she began to see the sincerity in my personality and my commitment to my future. The events of my pregnancy drew us closer than ever before and life once again felt safe. The house was calm and peaceful without the insanity of my addiction. When we heard my daughter's heartbeat, all anger faded in my mom and she surrendered to the delight of a new baby.

I didn't participate in any support group or therapy sessions during this time of abstinence from drugs. I cut out all using friends and returned back as best I could to an average teenage life. My passion for motherhood inspired me fully. Even in the womb, my Laila was power enough to motivate me toward a better life.

On Monday evening August 24, 1998, at 8:17 p.m., my daughter Laila was born. She was bright-eyed and alert, full of smiles and energy. Laila's image at birth was a perfect reflection of my experience during pregnancy. Looking back, I was appropriately naïve to the demands of a newborn child. Being only a teenager myself, I had formulated unrealistic expectations about what it was going to be like as a mother. Throughout my pregnancy, I excitedly awaited with high hopes the fulfillment of these expectations. I expected bliss and wholeness. I thought my child would give me the love I was lacking within myself. I had imagined Laila bringing joy and happiness to my every waking moment. My sixteen year old logic told me she was going to "fix" me, make me better, and give me reason to live.

What an unbearable burden to place upon a newborn baby! However, Laila was spared the agony of having to be her mother's happiness because I quickly realized my thinking errors. The entire picture I had developed in my head of life as a mother was inaccurate and backward. I had not foreseen a helpless infant with total dependence upon me. I had not considered little sleep or constant care. I had been wrong in placing my expectations on Laila to fill me with the love I desperately sought. Whereas I was waiting for her to love me, I found quite the opposite happened—I had to love her! I formed the erroneous idea that I needed her but the truth was she needed me! The realization that a newborn infant is entirely incapable of meeting the emotional needs of the parent shattered me. It was not Laila's job to make me happy or whole. Those were qualities I was meant to develop within myself prior to becoming a mother. That way, I could pass these useful skills on to my daughter.

Having come to the conclusion that my expectations were unrealistic and impossible, I was left bitterly disappointed. Depression engulfed me once again as the realization set in, and I was left with the same familiar emptiness. Nine months of joyful anticipation came crashing to a painful end. I had to care for my young child without reciprocation. I had to give in ways I didn't feel capable of—with unconditional love, undivided attention, and unlimited time. I felt deeply lost and inadequate.

It was in this state of mind that I came upon an old friend while I was getting fuel at the local gas station. Laila was eight weeks old and it was the week before Halloween. Me and Joey stopped and talked for a bit, exchanging numbers before parting ways. Although Joey had been a part of the old drug gang, he wasn't there the night I was beaten; the last time I had been seen in the neighborhood. I knew he had asked about me after it happened, to check on me and see if I was okay. The truth is I liked Joey. I found him kind and attractive. We hadn't spent much time together in my cocaine days and I had never used drugs with him so I found him safe and intriguing. Plus, it had been a year since I had any contact with the people I used to do drugs with so I saw no threat in reconnecting with him. A few days went by and I called Joey.

We easily fell into a comfortable relationship. Our personalities were compatible and we cared for each other. He lived nearby and we spent a lot of time together. It was only a few weeks before I discovered that Joey was still on drugs, except now he was addicted to heroin. I liked cocaine because it eradicated the depression I battled internally. I saw no other reason to take drugs aside from boosting my mood. I didn't have an interest in other substances, especially depressants, as I figured that would only compound my emotional sadness. But hanging with Joey every day, I began snorting heroin. It was less expensive than cocaine so we used more frequently. I never liked the effects of heroin—the nodding out, the lethargy, the lack of functionality. My flavor was the polar opposite. I enjoyed the increase in efficiency and sense of elation produced by cocaine. What I did find useful about heroin was its assistance in alleviating the discomfort of coming down from cocaine. I found out something else about heroin rather quickly—it was physically addictive. Snorting heroin daily for a few short weeks built up a tolerance and a dependence on the drug. I now woke up sick in the morning if I didn't have dope. I now lived in fear of withdrawal. Physical dependence combined with mental obsession drove me to desperate measures in order to maintain my habit. I quickly fell back into the old life, only worse this time because I needed the drug to physically be well in my body. With Joey's drug knowledge and my resources, we progressed in active addiction. I became a slave to heroin and my every waking moment centered on the drug.

All my old behaviors returned. I was stealing from my family, cutting school to go to the city, and lying to everyone who knew me. I was using drugs at work and in class. I had drugs on me at all times. My mother was taking responsibility for my daughter because

I was unable to properly care for her, as I was barely managing my own life. I manipulated my friends to borrow money and their cars. I conned teachers into allowing me to skip assignments while passing the class. Three months into a heroin addiction, at seventeen years old, I was helpless, hopeless, and lost. I wanted to stop every day but found I could not break the vicious cycle on my own. I prayed for God to end the addiction. I cried and hoped and tried and worried. I sobbed endlessly through the night as I watched my Laila sleep, wondering what was wrong with me. I could not pull myself together for my own daughter. As much as I loved her, as much as I wanted to be her mother, the force of addiction overwhelms even the most sincere desire. My love for Laila was not enough to get me clean this time. I didn't know what to do. I saw no solution and no way out. For the first time in my life, I wanted to stop but could not. I became severely depressed as I failed each day in my attempt to stay clean. I gave up my fight to live and used more to cover the desperation I was feeling. Joey didn't want to stop while I didn't think it was possible. Together, we kept each other sick and locked in denial.

I entered an outpatient hospitalization program for depression. During one session, I broke down and confessed that I could not stop using drugs. Still being underage, the therapist immediately called my mom and she quickly arrived at the facility for a family meeting. I walked into the waiting area where my mother was sitting and marched bravely to her side. Looking directly into her eyes, I said, "Mom, I have a heroin problem and I need help." It was here, at this moment, in the lobby of a treatment center, where my mother's arms once again provided every ounce of inner strength and courage that I needed to stay alive.

The Struggle for Recovery

$\mathcal{N}$ow seventeen years old, with a five-month-old daughter, I entered into my first detox center. I stayed at Keystone less than a week as my insurance provider would only cover medical detoxification treatment but not rehabilitation. I was connected with an outpatient psychologist in the city who specialized in addiction and eating disorders. It was Julie, my new therapist, who suggested Narcotics Anonymous. At one of our first sessions, she gave me the NA Basic Text. This book contains the key information regarding the twelve-step fellowship. Chapters such as "Who Is an Addict," "Why Are We Here," and "How It Works" explain the foundation of the recovery program in Narcotics Anonymous. The second half of the book includes the personal stories of individual members. It is a comprehensive, informative text written by addicts and for addicts.

Within a week of leaving detox, I was using with Joey again. One sleepless evening, I lay in bed tormented by obsession and guilt, a state of mind common and familiar to me. For some reason, I opened up the NA Basic Text and started reading. I could not believe the contents of this book. The clear and profound explanation of the characteristics of addiction astounded me. I spent the entire night, wide awake, mesmerized by nearly every line of this book. How could someone know me so well? Who told the authors my innermost thoughts, my secrets, my hidden shame? The Basic Text so accurately described me that I experienced a spiritual awakening: there was hope. Others were just like me and had gotten better. An overwhelming sense of hopeless despair had crept over me in the few months of actively using drugs again. I saw no way out of my drug problem—with all my will and desire and effort, I simply was unable to stop. Yet now, I read in the pages of this book, there is a solution. An immediate relief overcame me when I realized that others shared my pain and had found the answer. Now I knew what was wrong with me. There was a name for my malady, finally: I was an addict.

Two books up to this time in my short life had had the remarkable effect of inspiring dramatic change in my overall well-being. There was Brian Weiss' *Many Lives, Many Masters*, which I read when I was fifteen. That was the first mind-altering book I came across, which opened my mind and life up to the possibility of something completely out of my realm of experience. Next, there was the NA Basic Text. This book planted the first seed of hope by piercing through a level of depression that even psychiatrists could not mend. In a single reading, my life was transformed. If others could do it, so could I. I would attend these meetings that were so often mentioned by members in the book. I contacted the twenty-four-hour hotline to inquire about the location and times for the next meeting in my area. I was passionate and excited: I had a plan, a way out of this horrible addiction.

The first Narcotics Anonymous meeting I attended was at 11:00 p.m. on a Saturday in Levittown, Pennsylvania. Filled with enthusiasm, I carried the Basic Text into the meeting room. I saw about six other people sitting in a circle. Never one for being shy, I approached and asked if this was the NA meeting. Keen on recognizing a newcomer, I was greeted warmly and introduced to all. Then a huge, towering man approached me, arms open wide. This man was probably seven feet tall and bigger than a football player. And he was reaching out to hug me. This strange affection was awkward and I didn't understand why this man was hugging me. I didn't know his name and he had never met me prior to this moment. Yet his embrace was comforting and warmth flowed into my heart. I felt loved.

I quickly discovered that hugs are the commonplace greeting in Narcotics Anonymous. I began attending meetings frequently as I learned more about the program. The "fix" I had hoped for in NA was not happening. Attending meetings with a supportive group of recovering addicts was supposed to make me better yet I still continued to use drugs. I could not stop, even after being exposed to a solution. Heroin had a tight grip on my ability to choose freely. Although I desired to be clean, I repeatedly picked up drugs, over and over again.

For a year and a half, I struggled on this way. Attending meetings, using drugs, trying to get clean, not wanting to give up heroin. The battle raged inside of me. I felt desperately hopeless and lost, broken inside. The continuous failure lowered my hope and self-esteem to non-existent levels. Addiction being progressive, I rapidly spiraled into unforeseen depths of darkness and devastation.

I did not find it easy to simply stop using drugs. The program of Narcotics Anonymous will not work unless I stop using first and I was unable or unwilling to do so. There is a saying in NA that "some have to die so that others can live," meaning that sometimes the death of a close loved one awakens us to the true reality of our disease. Addiction is fatal. My thinking was so full of despair that I heard that saying and decided I was one of those who were going to die in order for another to live. I resigned myself to the fact that I was simply unable to stay clean. Yet there were some major key components of the program that I was not incorporating into my daily life. There were supports and tools and suggestions that I was not utilizing. NA will work, if I work the NA program. Something inside of me knew that this was the only way out of addiction, so I did not want to leave the program. Instead of withdrawing my involvement in meetings and ending my relationship with my sponsor, I continued to actively try. One of my deepest fears was failure, so I did not want to let anyone in NA know how bad I was struggling, how hard I found it to get and stay clean. So I lied to everyone about everything. While I thought nobody knew, others in recovery can easily spot deception. They all knew.

I would come into meetings, so full of dishonesty that I would collect thirty- or sixty-day clean time key tags after I had just used drugs in the bathroom of the meeting location. I plastered a fake smile on my face and told everyone that everything was great, my life was really good and I was doing wonderfully. I would sit in the back of the room with the cute boy and pay no attention to the speaker. I would bring my young baby to the meetings in order to further convince others of my stability in recovery. I would share that things are going well for me and I was finally happy. The instant my mouth opened to speak, a lie would spill forth. Nothing about me reflected honesty and I didn't know how to change that. I would hear others tell me, "If nothing changes, nothing changes." Yet I couldn't be honest, I couldn't show others how broken I was, I couldn't admit I needed help. And I continued to use drugs, to suffer, and to destroy my life and those around me.

Because had I been able to tell the truth it would have gone something like this: I cry myself to sleep every night, rocking in the fetal position, full of self-hatred and guilt beyond belief. I would have said I was dying inside and I knew it. The light of my soul had flickered out and I was consumed with the evils of addiction. I would have told the people in NA that I was going to be sleeping in a car that night in North Philly, with a guy named Tavi that I had met only three hours ago. I would have said that my mother kicked me out of the house and I am not allowed to be alone with my infant child. Maybe I would have even told the truth about my mental state: I hated being me and I wanted to die.

There were overdoses. The first time I was found in my bed at my mom's house. Laila had already fallen asleep next to me while drinking her nighttime bottle. I had snorted heroin before lying down to go to sleep that night and woke up in the emergency room, strapped to an ambulance gurney. I remember six tremendous angels perched in the corners of my room. I saw one stir Laila awake by tapping repeatedly on her arm. I found out the details of what happened later. Upon being awakened, Laila had begun to cry. Being incapacitated, I was unable to respond. My daughter's cry woke up my mother, who was curious as to why I was not consoling my baby.

Breaking down my locked bedroom door, she quickly realized her answer. I was blue and not breathing. The ambulance came and was able to resuscitate me with the aid of Narcan, a powerful antagonistic medicine used to block the effects of opiate overdose and restart the heart.

In utero, Laila was able to steer my life onto the right track. Now as an infant, she was saving her mommy's life again. One would assume that would be enough, that with the experience of death I would quit using and finally begin a program of recovery. But a few months later, I again came to consciousness in the emergency room after heroin came close to taking my life for a second time. I had overdosed in the bathtub late one evening. My youngest brother was watching television in the other room, and the rest of the family members were sleeping. He made mention to my mother that I was in the bathroom for a very long time and it was very quiet. This is what addiction does to a family: *my twelve-year-old brother knew to be concerned for his sister's life.* When my mom went in to check on me, I was underwater but still breathing. The EMTs, now probably familiar with my address, responded quickly. I was again saved from being a statistic.

The inability to be honest with others kept me locked into addiction, and my disease progressed rapidly. In my senior year of high school, I was caught with cocaine in my purse and my locker. The high school administration had been working with my family for numerous years, through my previous drop out, then pregnancy, and now my current drug addiction. This was 1999 and I assume now if that were to happen the police would be called. However, the dean had me come into her office and together we made a deal. In order to graduate with my class, I would have to agree to enter into a treatment facility directly after the ceremony. I immediately agreed and walked with my peers on graduation day. The majority of my classmates were excited about Senior Week in a foreign country or an island or even the Jersey shore. Me, my clothes were packed in a suitcase in my mother's car, as I headed to rehab.

I spent a few weeks in the inpatient house at Today, Inc. before moving onto outpatient care. I was unable to stay clean and stopped attending sessions. While pregnant, I had completed the necessary preparations for entering college and had selected a university to attend in the fall. I used heroin the entire summer before beginning classes at Drexel University. During this time, life continued to get worse until I completely fell apart. My mother would purchase a monthly train pass for me to get to and from school but I was rarely able to make it to campus. I could not get past the North Philly stop without getting off the train. I tried to close my eyes so I wouldn't see it, listen to headphones so I wouldn't hear it announced, read a book so I wouldn't focus on the trigger. But I always exited the train and walked to the corner where I purchased drugs. I couldn't keep up with classes while trapped in a full-blown heroin addiction.

By the end of my first trimester at Drexel, it was clear that I could not remain enrolled at the school. I went to my professors and explained the situation: I was caught in a drug addiction, was unable to complete the class, and was checking into a long-term treatment center. The teachers were compassionate and understanding. I withdrew from all of my classes. Such ended my career at Drexel University, along with an eighty percent, five-year academic scholarship.

Christmastime of 1999, I checked into Livengrin detox. I was now an adult, at eighteen years old, and Laila had turned one in August. I stayed in Livengrin for medical detox only, as my insurance company would not pay for rehab at that facility but would cover another center about four hours away in Williamsport, Pennsylvania. So the day before New Year's Eve, my mom and my aunt drove me out to White Deer Run, where I would spend the next five months. I went through the rehab program, then transferred to the partial program, and finally moved into the women's halfway house. It was an intensive, long-term treatment plan that provided a solid basis for recovery. While in the partial program and the halfway house, I attended outside meetings and had a sponsor. I worked in the community and had recovering friends in the area.

The benefits of White Deer Run were twofold: the location of the facility placed me two hundred miles away from my drug-addicted friends, therefore removing all people, places, and triggers from my life. I was then able to clear my head enough to learn how to stay clean and recover. I had the opportunity to live in recovery and experience what that meant. I was in a safe and supportive environment where I could work through anger, fear, worry, and remorse without turning to drugs. I allowed the process of healing to take place without interfering with it by putting a substance into my body. Being such a distance from home, I could start a new foundation without distraction. It was the blessing I had been praying for.

I came home the end of May 2000, confident and ready to take on the world. I immediately returned to meetings and found a new sponsor. While in treatment, my previous sponsor had only been temporary because we both knew I would not be residing in the area for an extended period of time. Now home, I had to build a new recovery network. I attended meetings every day and called my sponsor daily. But I was not adjusting to the transition very well. Shortly after being home, I saw Joey. Actually, I was secretly seeking him out. I wondered about his well-being and wanted to know how he was doing in life. He was still using heroin, harder than ever. A few days later, I relapsed with him after being clean and living in recovery for over five months. I was devastated. I had wrongly assumed invincibility. I thought I would be immune to relapse after having so much time away from it. I thought I was better.

The next three months were hellish torture. I now knew there was a different way to live—I had experienced the gifts of recovery! I had felt joy, accomplishment, purpose, and direction. My eyes had once again sparkled. I had rediscovered dreams and set future goals. I not only knew I didn't have to live in active addiction, I didn't want to after tasting the sweetness of recovery. Life in relapse was intolerable. Joey and I were arrested buying drugs in the city, a charge I later had expunged. My mother, so enthused about my return home, was again baffled and shocked by my destructive behavior. My family life was in constant turmoil. I was lying, stealing, and manipulating again. The addiction lifestyle had returned full force and I was quickly beaten down to the point of utter despair.

I longed for freedom again, having known it was possible. I had had enough. I wanted to stop. I was willing to do whatever was necessary for me to get and remain clean. Another rehab was not realistic; I had just left long term treatment. I would have to do this with NA. With the gift of desperation, I was ready to change.

The First Year

It was on Saturday, August 19, 2000, when drugs entered my body for the last time. I didn't know I was to stop the next day and remain in recovery for the next nine and a half years. In fact, I had no faith in my ability to recover. Not an ounce of personal willpower was involved in ending active addiction for me. It was as if God had smiled down on me and allowed me access to a power source previously unavailable. For over a year and a half, I had been desperately trying to stop, yet inevitably found myself intoxicated again. This recurring failure had engrained a strong sense of doubt and hopelessness within me. Yet in spite of my fears and uncertainties, a remarkable change began to occur. I was somehow *not* picking up drugs.

Early in the evening that Saturday in August, my family left for our annual week of vacation in Wildwood, New Jersey. I had always loved Wildwood. For as long as I had been alive, my family and all my relatives spent the same week together down the shore every year. I have only fond memories of fun and playfulness, adventures and joy during our beach trips. It was a break from the chaotic influence of my father's growing alcoholism and the tension building in our home. Wildwood was my safe haven—my God spot.

This year, I was allowed, or forced, to go along because my mother was not willing to let me stay in the house while she was not there. I was actively using drugs and she knew the safety of her belongings would be at risk if I was left unattended in the home. Not knowing what else to do, she took me down the shore.

I thought I had packed enough cocaine and heroin to get me through most of the week. When the last of the cocaine was gone before the first rest stop on the Atlantic City Expressway, I was terrified and panicky. Because I was physically addicted to heroin, I greatly feared running out. Worry plagued me as I wondered how I was going to get drugs in Wildwood. I knew no one and had no transportation back to Philly. Not knowing what else to do, I prayed.

Later that evening, I called my NA sponsor and explained my crisis. I asked for help and soon she and another NA member were checked into the hotel across the street. They could only stay one night, as both had work early Monday morning. But before my sponsor left on Sunday afternoon, I had a local meeting list in my hand, my daily meeting selected, and directions to everyone. I didn't believe it would last or work, but I had to make one more attempt to save my life.

August 20, 2000, four days before Laila's second birthday, marks the anniversary of my clean date in Narcotics Anonymous. I detoxed on the beach of Wildwood—sweating, shaking, sleeping in the sun and sand. It was here that I began a 90-in-90, making a meeting every day for ninety days in a row. I attended a meeting every single night while on vacation, even on the evening of Laila's birthday party. And for the first time, I sat in the front row. I was a newcomer in a new area and people reached out to me with intense love and support. I found the courage to share—honestly. Perhaps the comfort and safety I had come to associate with Wildwood contributed to my ability to let down my guard and show my true feelings. Once I opened up my innermost self, the emotions poured forth in a continuous stream of tears. Relief flooded over me.

I think I cried for nine months straight, literally. The repressed pain and guilt had been unlocked and overwhelmed me in the early stages of growth. I've come to know this as a healthy, natural, and appropriate response to the adjustment into recovery, but at the time, I feared the grief would never end. Without the drugs numbing the pain I had initially attempted to suppress, old hurts rose to consciousness. The abandonment I had been afraid to face when my dad left, the rejection I buried with my first heartbreak; all these feelings came to the surface, begging to be acknowledged and released.

Sadness seeped out of my pores as I was cleansed of the depression and loss trapped inside of me. I sat in meetings sobbing as I healed from the hurts of addiction. I craved nurturance, love, and inspiration, and I found these needs being fulfilled by the gentleness and sincerity of the women in NA.

For many years, I returned to Wildwood during the week of my anniversary, to celebrate the joy of staying clean with the people who brought me back to life. I was only in town for the first six days of my recovery, yet to this day, I maintain the friendships forged during that painful week. That's what the power of Narcotics Anonymous does—it turns a dying seed into a blossoming flower with the reward of watching it grow.

Now with a week clean, the longest I had stayed away from drugs since returning home from White Deer Run, my family and I loaded up the minivan and headed back to Croydon, my hometown. I went directly to a meeting with my sponsor and shared in the group. Fully doubtful I would stay clean for very long, I woke up every single morning convinced that this would be the day I was going to mess it up. Today I was going to get high again and disappoint everyone because that's what I always did. For at least a month, I went to bed every night in utter shock that I had not yet gotten high. Day after day, I amazed myself when another day ended and I was falling asleep clean. I did not trust this recovery one bit because I was so used to relapse.

It began to dawn on me that there was a connection between this newfound ability to stay clean and the tools I was using in my life. Being unemployed, I was attending meetings once or twice a day. On the weekends, there was a group of us that would attend the morning, afternoon, and evening meetings together. We started to see each other constantly and began to carpool for our weekend meeting marathons. I would attend the same meetings each week so that people would recognize me. Sometimes, someone would even remember my name, making me feel worthy and valuable. I was sitting in the front of the meeting, near the chairperson and speaker, which minimized distractions so I could pay full attention. I was raising my hand and honestly sharing about myself, especially my doubts about this program working for me. Meeting attendance built the foundation of my recovery, as it is the basis for the fellowship.

I was also building a network of friends. Now in 2000, in Bucks County, there was not an abundance of teenagers getting and staying clean like myself. My support group developed into friends and parental figures usually much older than me. I found this to be to my advantage. The men and women I connected with and learned from had wisdom, experience, and maturity I did not. Some had used drugs for longer than I had been alive. Some had gotten clean before I was born. They saw hope in me entering recovery so young and wanted to pass on to the next generation what they had gained from recovery. I am grateful for the members who have become my lifelong mentors and companions. They have attended my college graduations and Laila's birthday parties. They have known me since I was a mere seventeen years old, first arriving in NA. Even today, many friends from those early years remain consistent in their solid support and friendship. I am aware that the lack of young people in recovery has changed. It is refreshing to see so many young faces breaking the cycle of addiction early and obtaining lifelong freedom.

I had to select a home group, a meeting I faithfully attended every single week. I choose an 8:00 p.m. meeting on Friday night in Langhorne, Pennsylvania. My home group members asked me to come early to help set up the room, put out literature, make coffee, and greet the newcomers. I couldn't believe how simply arranging furniture and cleaning up the kitchen provided such a sense of accomplishment. I developed self-worth and experienced productivity as I sat in the room I had helped organize. I became involved with others who were committed to service and fellowship. They became my friends as we stacked chairs and washed dishes together, discussing our families and activities. My home group relied on me to be there and taught me responsibility. I showed up, no matter what. Integrity calls for no excuses.

I was calling my sponsor every single morning, with a daily plan for the day. This was difficult for me because I always feared not knowing what to say. I found that I only had to start with, "Hello," and she took over from there. Even more astonishing, I was calling her outside of our regular scheduled time, like when I was thinking about drugs or wanted to contact Joey again. My sponsor started talking to me about step work and I began reading NA literature every night. I developed the habit of praying on a regular basis.

I came to see that there was a strong link between taking the suggestions of the program and having the ability to stay clean. It was through this process of repeated action that I realized something profound. I honestly credit my staying clean to me doing a 90-in-90. At the end of those ninety days, I experienced a definite miracle. Habitual patterns had been broken. I could clearly contrast the old me against the recovering me. I was no longer convinced that I would fail in recovery. I no longer carried around a deep feeling of hopelessness. I didn't even go to bed surprised to still be clean. I believed in the power of NA to support me in making positive changes. After ninety days of immersion in NA, a life-altering, miraculous understanding came to me: I could recover!

I must not make light of exactly how tremendous this realization was for me. Going from a state of hopelessness and failure to sudden belief in my capabilities provided the springboard that launched my commitment to NA. I was confident in the program's ability to assist me in personal growth and maturity. I had finally been placed on the basic level of human survival: I wanted to live. If that was all NA was able to offer me, I would have been content right there. I had arrived on the playing field of life. Little did I know, the potential I foresaw was miniscule compared to what God had planned. The possibilities waiting to be embraced were endless.

Long before I ever picked up a drug, I felt the "uns" and "ins" of alcoholism: unloved, unworthy, unheard, and unrecognized. Inadequate, insecure, incapable, and invisible. I longed to be put together, as if I were Humpty Dumpty. I had always felt broken. This inner sense of inferiority led me to conclude that there was something wrong with me. Not something wrong with my life or my current problems or my family or personal circumstances. No, it was *me*—there was something inherently wrong with who I was as a person. I did not consider myself a human being who had made mistakes. I believed I was the mistake.

It was clear to me that although drugs became my problem; they had started out as my greatest solution. Now that I was committed to staying clean, I knew I had to address the problem of "me" or I would return to using again. I was constantly uncomfortable in my own skin. I couldn't stand the idea of being with myself without something to relieve the burden of disgust that I carried around. If I didn't do something to "fix" the way I felt about myself, I was sure to return to drugs again.

In Narcotics Anonymous, I heard that the "steps are the solution and the problem is me." This was exciting for me because there was no way I would stay clean without releasing the self-hatred and self-centeredness that drove my life. I longed for self-acceptance, to live in a world where it was good to be me. My sponsor pointed me in the direction of step work.

The first thing I did was determine what I wanted. What was my ideal picture of Life for Sara in Recovery? Who did I want to be and where did I want to go? These were extremely difficult questions for me because I had *no* clue. I didn't even know what my favorite color was let alone where I wanted to be in five years. I was nineteen years old, had a two-year-old daughter, and had spent the majority of the last five years insane on drugs, or in treatment. I had no self-identity and no idea how to develop one. My growth and development had been grossly halted.

It took some discussion, reflection, thought, and explanation, but I was able to pinpoint a basic description of the purpose of recovery, goals for recovery, and ideal recovery. I will state now that this was the most important exercise I did in early recovery. Having no relationship with myself at all, I felt overwhelmed and confused by the assignment. Yet it provided an introduction to "me." After years of self-destruction, I really wanted and needed to connect with a hopeful, promising part of myself. At nineteen years old, here was my vision:

Purpose: In the beginning, staying clean was the only purpose of recovery for me. It was simple and clear: the whole reason NA was in my life was to ensure that I did not return to drug use.

Goals: These were more difficult and I could only come up with one thing I hoped to achieve in recovery. I wanted to be in the state of mind where even if I were to be offered unlimited quantities of cocaine, I'd have no desire to put it into my body. The state of being where it is so good to be me that even without *any* consequences, I would still decline cocaine because I would not be interested in changing who I was. I imagined my response to be, "No, thank you, it's simply too wonderful to be Sara today and I do not want to hurt her." A state of living where being me is better than enough, it's perfect.

Ideal: my vision of an ideal recovery involved using the tools of NA, taking suggestions, making meetings, sponsorship, and working the twelve steps. It included enjoying recovery maintenance—not because I had to but because I wanted to.

When I was initially coming off drugs, it was a time of extreme discomfort on every level. It was basically impossible for me to sit still, especially through an hour and a half meeting. I fidgeted constantly, sitting on my hands, stretching my legs; there was an incessant need to move. I was jumping out of my own skin. I bit my nails and cuticles until they bled. I had something in my hand and mouth at all times. Whether it was gum, my fingers, a cigarette, food, or a water bottle, I was frantically trying to appease my oral fixation. I was anxious and scared, seeking stability and comfort. It was awkward, painful, and uncomfortable to be me without drugs. I used to sit in NA meetings and look around the room at other people, longing to trade places with them. I would have given anything to live their lives instead of my own. It was not that I necessarily wanted what they had; I didn't even have to know the person. The point was that it just hurt so bad to be me.

Now that I was sharing honestly and letting others help me, people in the rooms of NA would tell me to persist. This is why consistent meeting attendance is the key to recovery. Others used to be just like me—anxious, fearful, depressed—but found freedom through the steps. I knew they were telling the truth because you can't hide peace. They radiated with serenity, therefore, I trusted them. I was convinced. I readily committed to working the NA steps with my sponsor. I couldn't wait to begin feeling better so I started immediately. I didn't know I was about to embark upon a journey of intense mental, emotional, and spiritual healing. Physical health was only the first improvement needed. The dramatic and transformational process of the twelve steps is profound enough to warrant a chapter of its own.

Step Work

Step One: We admitted that we were powerless over our addiction, that our lives had become unmanageable.

The first key concept in the first step is powerlessness. This was a word I understood and acquainted strongly with hopelessness. I often wondered why, after adamantly vowing to not use again, I found myself high once more. Nightly, I prayed for the drug use to end, only to care less about my commitment in the morning. I tested myself daily to see if I could beat the addiction.

Laila's day care center was a single block from my mother's house. I could look out my bedroom window and see the building. Every single evening, I prayed desperately for God to grant me the ability to get my daughter to daycare before I got high. I knew there was no hope for me not to use; my thinking centered on harm reduction. Just let me get Laila to school first. I may have been able to do it three or four times in the five-month period of living at my mom's house. I just could not prioritize properly: drugs ruled me. I would wake up dope sick, needing heroin. It took everything in me to get us ready and out the door in the morning. Once in the car, auto pilot took over and we headed directly to the city. I was driven only by the need to relieve my sickness. I knew how to get well and I had to do that as soon as possible.

The two primary characteristics of addiction are obsession (overwhelming desire) and compulsion (inability to stop). Regardless of my prayers, hopes, or wishes, I was unable to keep Laila safe. No matter how much I tried or wanted to act differently, addiction controlled me. Yet I loved Laila enough to continue to attempt, morning after morning, to control when I used. The longer I repeated this pattern, attempting to exert control over addiction, the more hopeless I became. This is the process through which I ended up associating powerlessness with hopelessness. If I had no power to change it, it could not be changed. There was no hope.

The second important concept of unmanageability was also painfully obvious to me. I knew other teenage girls were not living the way I was. I could plainly see the disaster of my life by comparing the level of normalcy between me and other kids my age. I made a list. Here is what was normal for my childhood friends: playing sports through high school, attending a two- or four-year college, working at a part-time job, having a few ex-boyfriends, planning beach trips in the summer and ski trips in the winter. Overall, my friends had a positive outlook on life with hopeful excitement for the future. Basically, they were maturing properly, experiencing and enjoying life. Here is what my history looked like: I had dropped out of high school and withdrew from college, had gotten pregnant and was a mother, was now not allowed to be alone with my child, did not know who my child's father was because of my promiscuity, was in and out of rehabs, had been kicked out of my house, had been arrested, stole from my employer, and knew Kensington and North Philly like my own neighborhood. Overall, I was hopeless and insane. Basically, I had no coping skills and experienced no personal growth or development.

When looking at the events of my past, I had to admit three glaring facts. One, addiction is clearly progressive. My life consistently got worse and will continue to do so until I end up permanently insane, in jail without parole, or dead. Those are the only three ways to end active addiction. Second fact, I qualified as an addict. Therefore, the NA program could help me. Third, I could not use successfully. Every failed attempt proved that I had no power over addiction. I now could face the facts and surrender in defeat. Addiction had me beat. When I put drugs into my system, I can't control what happens next.

Through the process of my first step, I began to see that unmanageability has two layers: outer and inner. The outer is the mess that others can see, while the inner is hidden only to me. Because I knew that most people did not sleep in abandoned cars in dangerous neighborhoods with homeless men, the outer dysfunction was easily recognized. Inner turmoil was harder and more uncomfortable for me to identify because it required a new level of honesty. It was difficult to share the feelings I secretly harbored within myself—the hopeless despair that had me attempt suicide at fifteen; the agonizing shame that had me crying myself to sleep each night; the empty void that had me bingeing and purging; the punishing guilt that had me cutting my arms; the desperate loneliness that had me sleeping with strangers; the terrifying fear that had me biting my lips and chewing my nails.

This is who I am left with when drugs are taken away from me. This is the internal dissonance that loved to get high. These feelings and behaviors had to be addressed so I could see the true nature of my addiction. It was awful, disgusting, and painful to acknowledge who I really am under the drugs. Exposing my absolute weakness leaves me vulnerable and open. Yet this is the paradoxical twist of Narcotics Anonymous: *the most powerful words an addict can state are "Help me. I hurt."*

Step Two: We came to believe that a power *greater than ourselves could restore us to sanity.*

Having given up the fight of addiction, I was no longer anguished by obsession. The exhausting struggle was over. I could not win so I was not playing the game anymore. Without the incessant stream of drug thoughts running through my mind continuously, I was left with *a lot* of open space and available time. My entire being centered on using. When addiction ended, it seemed I had an additional ten hours of free time in my day. I didn't know what to do with myself; I had to develop all new habits and hobbies. The giant space that used to occupy addiction—getting and using drugs—was now empty. This created an uncomfortable void within me, a sort of gaping wound. I felt open, exposed, and raw. And I was. Accepting that addiction no longer works for me and giving up the fight, removes the power struggle and leaves me vulnerable to relapse as I try to once again fill the aching void. This is precisely the point where addicts are susceptible to substitution—replacing one addiction for another but never dealing with the underlying issues. It serves to turn attention away from the inner loss and grief. Yet raw pain is part of the healing process. Give it time, at least a few months. Experience the freedom recovery has to offer through the steps prior to turning to doctors for immediate relief. Depression, guilt, restlessness, remorse, anxiety—these are common and appropriate feelings to be experiencing after ending an active addiction. Work a vigilant recovery program for ninety days and then decide if psychiatric attention is necessary. Nobody has the inner motivation to get out of bed after a brutal six-day cocaine binge. But that is not clinical depression; it is the body healing itself. I had to learn that it was okay to be uncomfortable. I had to begin to trust that all things will pass.

Drugs had been my best and usually only friend. They were my most utilized coping mechanism. Cocaine comforted me through sadness and heroin masked the pain of my tears. Together, they soothed my depression and gave me a semblance of temporary pleasure. Although drugs took away everything of value and importance, I had to recognize that I was giving up a part of myself that I had become very attached to. I clung to addiction as a distorted façade of love.

The insanity described in the second step is the constant overpowering desire and obsession to use drugs despite all the negative consequences it was creating it my life. Having identified the problem in the first step, I was now challenged to believe that I could experience freedom from the nonsense of my head. But I did not even know what freedom was because I was so familiar with my addictive thinking. I could not recall a time when I had other interests outside of using. I did not remember what I used to think about in my childhood before addiction took over. All I knew was that my whole life was geared toward getting and using drugs, and now that I was clean, I didn't know what else to replace it with or even how to begin to do that.

Here is where the second step comes in. My task was to define what sanity meant to me. I needed something that could help me be comfortable in my own skin and fill the empty void inside of me. That to me is restoration to sanity. Being okay with Sara wherever I am. Other people claimed to have been as crazy and obsessive as me, yet they were now clearly rational and sane individuals. I began to look for times when I experienced a shift in thought, feeling, or attitude.

There were moments when I would be trapped in my old ideas, thinking about giving up on recovery or hooking back up with Joey. Instead of acting on these thoughts, I picked up the phone first. There slowly developed a space between thought and action. My behaviors were no longer running on impulse: think = do. I started to share my ideas with others before actually doing anything. I began to see that after talking something through, the compelling nature subsided and I could make a rational decision. I was experiencing the restoration of sanity.

The second step began to sink in deeply during periods of obsession. I saw that I could attend a meeting, share honestly about what was going on, and leave that very meeting feeling entirely different. That was a profound miracle for me! To want, crave, and desire to do something and not end up doing it, was extraordinary in my eyes. It was like being talked off the ledge. Something was definitely working in this NA program, and I wanted more of it. I learned that when I was not feeling okay, I could use a tool of the program and very likely, begin to feel better. I realized why the people in NA were able to laugh and smile and play. They had been relieved of the burden of addiction; they knew how to work a program and were now free to enjoy life.

Over time, I came to experience the hope available in step two. I believed in the power of NA and the tools of the program to help me because I saw them working in my life. I had never faced my problems before because I did not believe there was a solution. In the process of working the second step, I came to realize that there is nothing I cannot get through clean. I could deal with the emotional pain because I knew how to handle it. I learned that at any given moment, anytime I find myself in an uncomfortable state, I could use one of the tools of the program to help me get through it. Sharing with my sponsor, calling a supportive friend in recovery, writing in my journal, praying, reading NA literature, participating in a meeting, doing service work, taking a walk, bike riding—these and countless other healthy coping skills became accessible. By practicing these skills in my daily life, I came to believe that I could get better, too.

The first step revealed to me that amazingly, I could stop using drugs. The second step showed me that even more than not using, I could recover like others had by working the NA program. It seemed to me that the rewards of staying clean were just getting better and better.

Then my world fell apart and my commitment to recovery was challenged. With about sixty days clean, I was ready to move onto my third step. I was radiant and glowing; alive with the hope that life was going to improve. At that time, I had three meaningful relationships in the program: my sponsor, Karen, who I talked to daily and who was taking me through the steps; my best friend, Laura, who was three years clean and lived four blocks away; and my boyfriend, Joel, a guy from NA who had gotten clean a few months ahead of me. With two months clean, these were the members of my support network. I spoke with all three of them daily, usually multiple times. Laura, Joel, and I did everything together. I was doing a 90-in-90 so we ended up at a meeting every day. We took road trips on Saturdays to distant meetings, baked cookies with Laila on Wednesday nights, attended recovery picnics, bowling events and went roller skating. We were young and having a lot of fun. I had friendships in a way I had not experienced since grade school.

One Saturday afternoon, Laila and I walked over to Laura's house for a visit. She wasn't expecting us but that wasn't unusual; we often showed up without notice. I would get bored and restless and need to get out of the house so we frequently arrived on Laura's doorstep unannounced. That afternoon, as Laila and I pressed the doorbell and waited for Laura to answer, I was the one in for a surprise. My boyfriend opened the door.

My first reaction was shock—maybe we had all planned to meet here like we sometimes did and I forgot. Maybe it was 6:00 p.m. on Thursday and I was showing up to carpool to our normal meeting together. It took all but a split second to recognize the absurdity in my thinking. A forgotten invitation was definitely not the case. My boyfriend was here specifically because I was not. I had been betrayed by the two people I was closest with in the whole world. In an instant, I lost my best friend and my boyfriend. Now they had each other and I was alone.

I didn't know what upset me more: losing the best girlfriend I had had in years or seeing that the man I trusted was dishonest. The devastation and horror broke my spirit. I couldn't even look into their faces as I took Laila's hand and turned away. Tears welled up in my eyes but I refused to let them see how badly I was hurt.

As we walked back home, the mental and emotional upheaval tormented me. This was just too much. My whole support group had been ripped out from under me. The unanswered questions churning in my brain had me furious and confused. How long had they been making a fool of me, smiling to my face and sneaking around behind my back? Were there signs I missed? Did I not notice the two of them flirting or sense their subtle lies? Could I have been so oblivious? The internal chaos had returned and I needed a release. I knew exactly how to escape the upset I was experiencing: I was getting high.

The instant we walked in my mom's front door, I went on a rampage. I frantically began scouring the house for anything I could use to get high—money, change, car keys, jewelry, electronics, a checkbook. On an addict's mission, I desperately flipped couch cushions, emptied desk drawers, turned over beds, and ransacked bureaus. I was in the old familiar compulsive frenzy. I was not stopping until I had a way to be high as soon as possible.

This whole time, my two-year-old Laila is following me around the house. With her tiny hands, she is holding her purple Teletubbies puzzle out to me. "Mommy, do this puzzle with me? Mommy? Please?"

My little toddler is learning to be polite and speak in sentences. This could have been a moment where I acknowledge her growth and instill a sense of accomplishment in my child's heart. Instead, I don't even make eye contact with her as I repeatedly exclaim, with great annoyance, "Not now, Laila!"

But my child is persistent. I was just about to tell her to go downstairs and leave me alone. The words were just about to leave my mouth. But it happened. I looked into Laila's eyes. It is important to understand that my child was born with the eyes of an angel. Incredible, crystal-blue mirrors reflecting heaven. As I turned to instruct Laila to go away, I was stopped dead in my tracks as the image of God appeared in her huge angel eyes. I fell to my knees and took Laila into my arms. Holding on to the only thing that has ever been able to save me, I begged God to take away the obsession to use. In that moment, I prayed like my life—and Laila's—depended on it. Because they did. I knew that if God didn't expel this desire, I was going to use again and die. I sobbed in anguish as I realized that would make Laila an orphan. Father: unknown. Mother: overdosed.

I don't know how long I cried with Laila on that living room floor but a peace came over me that I had never experienced before and have rarely since thereafter. The obsession had been removed; the crisis had passed. The disarray of the house would wait. Right now, I had a Teletubbies puzzle to do.

Step Three: We made a decision to turn our will and our lives over to the care of God as we understood *Him.*

As I moved onto the third step, I was radiant, glowing with hope for the first time. The second step had renewed my faith in the universe. Things were going to get better and I believed it. Now it was time for me to maintain trust in that universe to care and provide for me. The whole "let go, let God" concept baffled me. How does one develop a reliance on an unknown higher power and believe that that higher power cares enough to bring about only the best for me? How was I supposed to trust that this higher power is capable and willing to help me, to protect me, to guide me? The whole thing sounded mystical and strange. I didn't know how to do any of this or what any of it meant. Two things were of great assistance in clarifying my confusion. A useful suggestion by my sponsor and a personal awareness brought it all into perspective for me and the third step began to make sense in a realistic way.

As I was expressing my frustration with this "turning it over" concept, my sponsor encouraged me to make a "God Box." Here I would place all of my concerns, worries, fears, and problems before God. I found an empty tissue box and spent an afternoon coloring and decorating it. Every time I had something on my mind or in my heart, I would write it on a piece of paper and place it into the slit of my God box. It was a symbolic way for me to turn my will and life over to the care of God. It helped me tangibly see that I was giving up control over a situation. It reminded me that I was not allowed to worry or stress over things anymore because I had signed them over to the care of God. I gave my struggles to God to handle and He was working on resolving everything. I wasn't allowed to take anything out of the box but I could put the same concern in the box as often as I needed until I fully surrendered it. With practice, this act of giving up my worries calmed my mind and filled my heart with peace. A sense of trust and spiritual connectedness flowed through me.

I learned that I could choose to let go and trust instead of worrying and attempting to control. In fact, I was already doing so in many areas of my life. One example of my ability to turn things over occurred to me as I was dropping Laila off at daycare. Every single morning, I turned my daughter over to the care and protection of her teachers. I trusted them to a great extent—I did not fret or worry, stressing all day long over how they were treating her or what they were doing or teaching or playing with her. I had full faith and confidence in their ability to provide attentive, loving care to my Laila. I did not live in fear that my child would starve; I relied on the teachers to feed her. I did not agonize over the possibility of Laila crying, being left alone, abandoned, or neglected. I knew, without a doubt, that she was in the tender and kind care of gentle, loving, qualified teachers. Every morning, I easily surrendered the care of my own child to that day care, with faithful confidence in their ability to abundantly meet her every need.

Through this example, I began to see the parallel in my own life. I realized that I can and do trust higher powers all the time to work for me. Now I had to apply those principles of trust and faith to myself and my own powerlessness. Each day when I awoke, I made a conscious, spoken choice, through prayer, to give up my destructive, self-centered, fear-based will and offer my life in loving service to my Higher Power, whom I know as God. When I found myself again wrapped up in craziness, fear, or obsession, I simply remembered my decision to let God take care of every situation I encountered that day. When distractions pulled me away from being grounded in faith, as soon as I noticed, I returned my attention to the knowledge that, like Laila, I was in the loving care of a Power greater than myself. I'd say a million times a day, "God's got me." This walking prayer reminded me that God is always near and I no longer need to run the show of my life. Because experience showed me, I run it into the ground.

I may make this process of turning my will (my thinking) and my life (my actions) over to the care of my Higher Power sound simplistic and natural. The truth is that it was uncomfortable and strange and far from easy. Having very little experience in relying on trust versus living in fear, I often required outside support as I learned to lean on God. I could not yet get myself out of mental anguish on my own. Practicing the third step was difficult for me in the beginning because I was not good at surrendering my insanity—it was such an ingrained familiar part of me. What I usually needed in order to let go was a phone call to a friend, sharing at a meeting, or my nightly journal time. Sometimes, it would be hours or days before I even realized that I was holding onto anger, blame, depression, etc. It was frequently the loving reminder from friends that pointed out my forgetfulness. Like anything else though, I get better with practice. When the third step became an instinctual thought in my own mind, it was time for me to embark on a deeper journey.

Step Four: We made a searching and fearless moral inventory of ourselves.

After applying the third-step principle of trust consistently, I no longer had to be afraid of an inner cleansing. No pain was too great to bear with God and NA. I believed that, felt secure with that knowledge, and was ready for a fourth step. I now had to tell the truth. It was time to get to the heart of my pain and corruption, looking at myself directly in the eye. The fourth step gives me the flashlight to shine the refreshing, yet piercing light of day upon the dark secrets of my inner nature. To face my disgust and filth and acknowledge the shame of my past are not easy tasks to undertake. Unless I wanted to return to using, I could not avoid this vital step. It was time to review my personal history and be accountable to where my life had gone up to this point. If I wanted to create a new future, I had to accept full responsibility for the past so I could make different choices in the present. It would be necessary for me to let go of the blame game, squash my belief in entitlement, and identify my long-held patterns and motivations. I now had to address where my "good intentions" had led me astray.

This step has a reputation for being difficult and painful, dreadful even. Yet I saw this assignment differently. I had come to NA looking to "fix" a problem: my brokenness. The members convinced me that the steps were the path to self-acceptance and I desperately wanted to be comfortable in my own skin. The prospect of having a set of instructions to achieve my desired result thrilled me. The fourth step seemed like an invaluable piece of the healing process. I was excited to write it because I wanted to find out what was "wrong" with me and why I was the way I was: selfish and destructive, hell-bent on ruining my life. I sought freedom through knowledge and awareness; therefore, I took this step to be a key component on the path of self-realization.

However erroneous or immature my reasoning, it got me started on the life-altering process of the steps and motivated my soul-searching writing in the fourth step. Guided by a small booklet specifically designed as an outline for the fourth step, I began to answer the questions and write about my past. Topics included:

resentments, fears, relationships, sex, shame, abuse. Damage, demoralization, and immorality were focal points. Fresh out of the horror of active addiction, with about three months clean, it was painful to look at the causes of my addiction and conditions that contributed to my using. Yet that was precisely the best time to face it because I was still hurting on the inside and willing to do whatever I needed to do to feel better about myself. With the humbleness of humiliation and the desperation of devastation, I was in the perfect position to be rigorously honest about the present reality of my life. I had heard that this step was often accompanied by great discomfort, so I wanted it over as soon as possible. I was not going to be on this step for years as I had seen others do. It was the first time I had ever taken a personal inventory and it was an extensive work. I wrote every day for five months and experienced great relief when it was complete.

Side note: I know today, having done a variety of fourth steps, the process does not have to be agonizingly painful, simply truthful and direct. My first experience with a fourth step was through Narcotics Anonymous. In the years to come, I reviewed other issues in different fellowships. In 2002, I did a fourth step with my sponsor in Overeaters Anonymous, when I sought help for an eating disorder. In 2005, I used an Al-Anon sponsor to guide me through a fourth step dealing specifically with the effects of my father's alcoholism.

It's a privilege to have an indispensable tool such as the fourth step. It has value for people in everyday life as well as those with addictions. It has served a therapeutic and healing purpose at many different stages throughout my life. After a period, no matter how long, of immoral behavior and dishonest living, the fourth step is a necessary guide to realignment. Much like the Christian concept of confession, acknowledging my destructiveness breaks the bondage of guilt which binds me to the behavior. Then I am set free to live fully in the present.

An important aspect of the fourth step is also assets, those personality traits that are honorable and commendable, worthy of refinement and admiration. My sponsor had me make a list of those qualities that I did like about myself. After spending so much time focusing on the defective areas of my being, I was feeling rather overwhelmed and upset with who I had been. It was beneficial for me to get a balanced perspective. I did this by identifying characteristics, behaviors, or dreams within myself that I was proud of, enjoyed, or brought happiness to myself or others. This way, my inventory was complete. I could see clearly those aspects of myself that were useless and needed to be discarded while also recognizing what was valuable and worth keeping. In this light, I saw that I was a whole person, neither entirely morally corrupt nor one of heaven's angels. Having a rounded view of myself allowed me to see and accept me for who I was: a human being.

Step Five: We admitted to God, to ourselves, and to another human being the exact nature of our wrongs.

This was an overwhelmingly scary step for a perfectionist who was deathly afraid to admit mistakes to anyone out of fear of judgment. Yet the fifth step became the most liberating gift I've ever given myself. Having always sought the approval of others, sharing with someone all my past mistakes, secrets, relationships, shame, etc., was not high on my list of fun activities. In fact, I found it horrifying. Yet I knew I had to give my fourth step away. Holding on to it would waste my tremendous effort and I knew that if I continued to hold everything in, I would eventually use again.

As terrified as I was, I read my entire fourth step, completely and entirely, leaving nothing out. I found that I did not stun, shock, or even remotely surprise my sponsor. My deepest shame was met with her loving compassion. My paralyzing fears were comforted by her encouraging embrace as tears poured from my eyes during the difficult sections. I had dropped the mask of perfection and let somebody into my truest self. All the protective walls of anger came tumbling down. I took the biggest risk of my life by trusting another person. I vulnerably exposed those aspects of myself that I had hidden away—certain that if anyone knew, they would see how bad and dirty and wrong I was. Yet as I opened up to my sponsor, she responded with unconditional acceptance. When somebody else extended love to me so completely after seeing my immense weaknesses, I found comfort and acceptance that made it okay to be me. For the first time in my life, I felt a part of humanity instead of some horrible beast with no sense of belonging. I was a human being—with strengths and faults and that was okay because everyone else had them to! Finally, we were the same. I was simply and perfectly okay.

Ending the fourth step with a list of personal assets was instrumental for me. It had been hard to initially come up with positive traits about myself but actually sharing these characteristics with my sponsor was really difficult also. Accustomed to living with an overwhelming sense of guilt, it was a challenge to acknowledge, accept, and embrace goodness in myself. Almost as hard as having to admit all the wrongs I had done. I was therefore grateful to have assets to discuss at the end. After divulging hours of remorse and tragedy, I could conclude my fifth step with inspiration.

There were many good qualities about myself that I needed to identify and build upon, with the help of my Higher Power. Through the fifth step, the past no longer controlled me by default nor held me down unconsciously. It was like a fountain of clean water had washed years of mud and filth from me. I was elated upon completion of my fifth step, having released tremendous emotional blockages. I was now free to live for today, in the present moment, without the hindrance of the past. I was free to finally be me! Now, it was time to ask: who the heck was I?

Step Six: We were entirely ready to have God remove all these defects of character.

Having just faced the reality of my previous existence, I was able to identify some core characteristics that made me who I was—the inner motivations that drove my behavior patterns. This answered my life-long question of why I had done the things I've done. With the help of an insightful sponsor, I was able to recognize the falsehood of my operating principles: dishonesty, control, fear, anger, secrecy—just to name a few of my more glaring defects. It became apparent to me how often I responded to life with self-righteousness, hurt, and isolation. These immature reactions were hiding a lonely terror which resided inside of me that I covered up with poor defense mechanisms and harmful coping skills.

In the rooms of Narcotics Anonymous, they call this the "grow or go" step and it has earned its reputation for good reason. Identifying how my core defects show up in my behavior and feeling their painful consequences *hurts*! It is not pretty or fun when my failures and frailties are revealed to me. The process of becoming entirely ready often involves pain. I usually do not want to give something up if I still perceive it as serving a purpose. Letting go of harmful and destructive aspects of myself requires maturity, willingness, and support. It is a first step on a deeper level as I admit my powerlessness to change myself. The drugs are no longer an excuse because I am clean. Yet I find myself often making poor choices, still lying, and repeatedly acting in ways contrary to what I know to be right. And more than that, I find that no matter how much I want to or try to, I cannot stop these bad habits on my own. I continuously make the same mistakes over and over again, baffled as my willful attempts turn out to be futile. It is here, at this moment of honest frustration, that I must come face-to-face with a profound truth: I am the problem.

I was fed up with the awareness of my defects, with myself, with life, and with constantly relying on the same maladaptive behaviors that I knew no longer worked. I was sick of living in fear; I destroyed everything I touched. I felt completely out of control, totally insane, and powerless—all over again. I recalled the unmanageability of my first step when I was just getting clean and couldn't help but be horrified at the parallels in my current behavior. Except now I could not blame my impulsivity or self-centeredness on drugs. I had to take responsibility for who I was and how I lived.

Having just become aware of my dysfunctional nature, I often felt like a huge ball of defects, utterly useless in every way. I simply could not change these horrible traits or their accompanying harmful behaviors. Striving to relieve myself of my defects drove me into a state of suicidal depression. When I attempt to exert power over things I am powerless over, I end up hopeless and unmanageable. This was my experience with the sixth step.

I was a crazy mess as I was driving down I-95 on a Sunday afternoon. I had about a year and a half clean and was on my way to a meeting I attended regularly in South Philly. I had just ended a relationship with a boyfriend who wouldn't stop shooting heroin. That boyfriend was Joey, my ex from years before. Around my six-month anniversary, he had started to come to meetings. Of course, I was ecstatic and when he celebrated ninety days, we started dating again. I had nine months clean, was actively involved in recovery, working steps with my sponsor, and doing service at my home group. I had lost the obsession to use and was beginning to enjoy myself and my life. Joey was court stipulated to meetings and only clean so that he could pass drug screens given by his parole officer. When he used again and went to jail for five months, he asked me to stay with him and I did. I visited him in the county jail on weekends and wrote letters to him every day. I wanted to believe his story: he's learned his lesson, he's ready to change, he's sick of the addictive life, he's committed to recovery. Like many addicts, when clean, Joey is caring and protective, charismatic, and fun. I enjoyed getting to know this side of him even more as he was incarcerated and trusted he would continue to grow upon his release. That is not what happened.

When I found syringes in his pocket one night, I knew I had to go. My sponsor had been encouraging me to leave him but I wanted to believe he would change. He insisted he was clean and I would hear him talking to his sponsor. Denial, love, and fear kept me from saying goodbye. I believed that if I were in his life, at least I would know he was alive and in seeing me clean, maybe he'd want to get better too. Control and codependency were sure to kill me if I stayed. I knew better than to believe I could associate with using addicts and not return to using. I'd get high with Joey way before he got clean with me. My recovery was in danger. Having been trained well in NA, I understood that no relationship was worth compromising my recovery. It was time to move on without him.

Now driving to my Sunday night meeting, after just having ended the relationship with Joey, it all hit me. My defects were glaring in my face and I was overcome with grief. Had I not gotten any better in this entire eighteen months? Why did I not see through his lies from the beginning? How could I allow myself to care so much about someone so unavailable and unwilling? What was wrong with me? Why was I attracted to derelicts that I wanted to help change? I was right where I was when I got clean: an emotional mess, devastated and broken, lost and hopeless. I began sobbing uncontrollably, so hard that the tears were blurring my vision and I could barely focus on the highway. I saw a big yellow bus in front of me and I suddenly had a thought: I'll hit the bus and drive into the guardrail. This pain is too unbearable, I feel like I've gotten nowhere in recovery, I'm making the same stupid mistakes over and over, and I am simply overwhelmed with life. This breakup, these defects, being me—it was all so painful! Anything would be better than this…in fact, maybe using wouldn't be so bad after all.

Having the serious thought and slight desire to get high terrified me into a panic. It had been so long since that afternoon in my mother's living room when I broke down in the middle of an addictive frenzy. Now the craving for drugs had returned and I was very scared. I knew what I'd be losing if I got high but the pain of being me seemed too great to bear. I went to God and prayed. Finally, I bargained with myself: if I still wanted to hit a bus on the way home from the meeting, I'd get high instead. I rationalized that if my desire to die was still that strong, I'd turn to the lesser of two evils and get some cocaine instead of taking my life. I had money in my purse and was sure that in a year and a half I had not forgotten my way off the Allegheny Ave exit. This negotiated compromise satisfied me and I drove to the meeting. I still kept death and using an option, just as a decision meant for later. That later never came because that meeting saved my life.

As I walked into the church where the meeting was held, it was clear that I was in obvious emotional distress. My girlfriends in NA swarmed me with love and hugs and encouragement. Easily recognizing my despair and hopelessness, the old-timers insisted I sit in the front row and supported me while I shared my agony. A woman held my hand and rubbed my back the entire meeting. A girl with just a few days clean came up to me and told me it would be all right.

The atmosphere of recovery was present and this is how addicts stay clean. Pain shared is pain lessened. I walked away free.

A remarkable change occurred within me during the course of hugs, tears, conversation, and loving support. I gave my every character flaw to God. I let go, knowing I was helpless to ever make myself different or better. As the bond of unity flowed into my heart, it melted the terror, pain, and sadness. I emptied myself of the lost feeling of depression. I had once again surrendered, only this time on a much more profound and personal level. I realized here that I was powerless (unable) to change me without God's help. This opening allowed the glorious light of hope to shine in and fill my heart. I experienced relief.

It was a major turning point in my recovery as I cut the last tie to my using days. The decision and action to leave Joey was not easy, it was a great loss that I only got through with the amazing support of my sponsor and NA friends. I lived in meetings—crying, sharing honestly, and allowing myself to be comforted. It broke my heart to walk away from Joey, leaving him to be swallowed up by the waves of addiction, knowing it was only going to get worse for him. I'll never make Joey want recovery enough to work a program. I'll never be able to fix, manage, control, or change him. Although the potential may exist for him to one day become himself again, I realize that due to many years of active addiction, the person I know and remember Joey to be is not who he is today. Over a decade later, Joey has spent more than six years in prison and is currently only a few months into another lengthy sentence. Throughout the years, each time he goes away, I try to send him friendly letters of support. If there's anyone I'd like to see get and stay clean, it'd be Joey. The decision to end our relationship can be classified as one of the hardest things I've ever done but it just could have been the deciding factor in our two very different life paths. Time passed and the separation between me and Joey increased. As the consequences of his active addiction grew to horrendous levels, my life was about to take off in unforeseeable ways.

Step Seven: We humbly asked him to remove our shortcomings.

Character defects: the harmful, destructive aspects of one's personality

Shortcomings: the impulsive behaviors that arise in response to character defects

When the character defects are removed, the accompanying shortcomings vanish as well. Now free of the painful bondage of personality defects, I literally felt like a new person. I had a glimpse of the woman I was in God's eyes: perfectly fulfilled, whole, and complete. Dreams previously blocked by the defect of fear sprung to new life within me and I remembered who I was before I became afraid to live. I had the sense of a "self," of being a truly unique and special individual—who I truly was and always had been. I saw how I had repressed, denied, and betrayed myself for so long, that I forgotten and lost my identity. The seventh step gave me back me—free, unencumbered, and uninhibited. When the harmful defects such as control, fear, and inadequacy were removed, I discovered there was a person underneath all that mess! Even more than there being a person and not a giant ball of self-hatred, I realized I liked this girl. In fact, she was kind of great. I suddenly had an overwhelming desire to get to know myself. I enjoyed my own company and wanted to spend time with me! My sense of self had previously been built on trash—lies, facades, and false beliefs. The sixth and seventh steps cleared all that away, and I was now finding the diamonds that the mud had been covering. I was a jewel, a beautiful, glowing gem. This perspective is monumentally different than that of my old image which involved considering myself as a piece of dirty, used, broken garbage.

The journey of discovering me was an invigorating process of falling in love with myself. I learned new things every day as I became my own best friend. Being on a self-punishing mission my entire life, it was refreshing to find goodness and joy within me. As I came to value my life, my personal well-being became precious to me. I began taking care of myself on many new levels. I enjoyed waking up because I got to be me all day and that fact alone was enough to put a smile on my face. The seventh step allowed me to get to know me as God knows me. As I continue to grow in recovery, the awareness of who I am in God's eyes deepens and develops in greater humility. Some of the insight into myself as an individual is worth noting and will perhaps offer a miniscule peek into the enormous impact this step had on my life's direction.

I discovered that I loved the color blue, then changed to red, and now it's purple! I learned that I like my socks to match my outfits and at my best, my dress style is conservative and sophisticated. I cannot tolerate scary movies; Harry Potter gives me nightmares. Injustice on any level makes me furious. Massage and all forms of body work, such as acupuncture, chiropractic care, and reflexology, are my favorite ways to say I love you to myself. I get irritable when I am cold or wet and if combined, it escalates to meanness. I readily spend my disposable income on international travel, exotic beaches, and cultural landmarks because I want to see and experience the world. I would move to a new region and location every two years but my Laila prefers stability and familiarity so we stay in the general Philadelphia area. I'm a natural adventurer—hiking, bike riding, and being outdoors exhilarates me. If not pressed for time, I enjoy getting lost in new places and seeing where the road leads me. Tea parties with my daughter were my favorite spring play date when she was a toddler. My dream date would be a hot air balloon ride. I have an amazing gift of articulation and had I not been caught up in addiction as a teenager, should have seriously considered law school. I'd choose intelligent conversation over emotional romanticism every time. My preference is theater rather than movies. When I lay in bed at night, the last thing I say is, "Thank you, God."

I included that last paragraph to reveal just how much impact the seventh step had in freeing me to discover myself. Maybe regular or healthy people automatically know how to develop a relationship with themselves, grow into maturity, and effectively navigate life. Not being regular or healthy, I had none of these skills and had always felt ill-equipped to face and handle the responsibilities of adulthood. Through step work, I now sensed that I had gained at least one of the tools for successful living—knowing myself. I was beginning to experience real freedom—the freedom of choice.

My decisions reflected my newfound self-worth and I made many drastic changes in my life. At this time, I realized that I wanted to go back to college. I was twenty-one years old with two years clean when I quit my job at a local newspaper and enrolled full time at Bucks County Community College. This proved to be a decision that would set the course for my future. During the next seven years, I studied a plethora of topics, mostly esoteric in nature, and earned many degrees. Most importantly, I discovered my heart's passion was in education and inspiration.

Ongoing life issues that seemed ingrained and unchangeable shifted profoundly. Codependency transformed into personal responsibility as my fear of being alone was removed, and I no longer needed a man to validate my existence. I spent the next eight years as a strong, independent, single mother. Inadequacy was replaced with confidence as I came to trust myself, and I began to walk with my head held high, looking people directly in the eye because I no longer had anything to hide. My decade-long depression became a joyful attitude when I began to have hope in my future and my ability to achieve. I would awaken in the morning with a great sense of enthusiasm, simply because I was excited to live, finally engaged in life. I had always secretly thought there was a hint of greatness in me, but now—excellence radiated from my pores. Being alive was finally a beautiful experience.

Step Eight: We made a list of all persons we had harmed and became willing to make amends to them all.

This step appeared relatively simple to me. I review my fourth step resentment list to discover the part I played in all of my relationship problems. Taking full responsibility for my role, it now becomes necessary for me to own up to it. I immediately thought of the ninth step and fear crept in. Did this mean I was going to have to say I was sorry to people that I believed should be apologizing to me? No way was I going to do that! My sponsor pointed out to me in my moments of resistance that the eighth step only asks me to make a list and become willing. That means *possibly, if needed, somewhere down the line* I *may* want to clear up my wrongs. That was easier for me to do. I could write an honest list, pulling the names from my fourth step inventory. Together with my sponsor, we decided who should be on the list and who did not need to be there. Practically everyone in my life had been affected to various degrees by my active addiction and there was extensive clean up necessary. It was the second part of the eighth step that was trickier for me: becoming willing. Some of these resentments I had held on to my whole life and felt justified in doing so. Getting to a point where I wanted to correct the damage I'd caused was a challenge because in some relationships, I couldn't even see where I had been wrong. The process required rigorous honesty, group support and a lot of prayer. But the change was miraculous and the effect permanent. I soon found that the sixth step was prematurely deemed the "grow or go" step. The eighth step is the determining factor deciding those who mature into successful recovering adults and those who shrink from responsibility while regressing towards relapse.

There was one key relationship, my father, where I was unwilling to budge. Anger seeped from my pores at the simplest mention of his name. I was still playing the victim. The blame game was a deeply engrained pattern for me, and I refused to see that I played any part in our estrangement. In fact, it was my choice to exclude him from my life, and I felt fully entitled to that decision. He had failed in his duty as my father and I could see no redemption possible. I was harsh, bitter, and critical. At the mere mention of his name, I became tense, angry, and indignant. My physical reaction and emotional response clearly demonstrates how holding on to resentments deeply affects a person's core overall health and well-being.

For a good part of my childhood, my father was an unpredictable, mean drunk. I didn't like him. He scared me, he hurt me, he insulted me, and he embarrassed me. Most importantly, my father disappointed me. Over and over and over again. The man I wanted to treasure me and adore me repeatedly wouldn't even acknowledge that I existed. I used to have hope in him. As a little girl, my prayer was for my daddy to be happy and love me. I begged God nightly to let my daddy be a nicer person. After years of hoping for my dad to change, the open wound of disappointment hardened into anger.

I felt justified in my intense hatred of his inability to properly care, nurture, or provide for his family. I watched my mother exhaust herself, relentlessly, day after day, to compensate for my father's lack of parental participation. My mom worked long hours only to come home and make dinner, take us to practices, help with homework, get us washed up and into bed. There was no time for her to breathe, relax, or take care of herself. Because of my father's irresponsibility, my mother went overworked, underpaid, unappreciated, and exhausted for many years while meeting the outrageous demands of four young children on her own. Although my father lived in the house with us during most of my childhood, he was largely useless, being more of a burden than a support to my mom. She took care of us entirely: physically managing our active sports schedules, financially being solely responsible for our needs and education, emotionally responding to our childish upsets. My father's alcoholism placed overloaded responsibilities on the whole family, but most specifically, I watched the effects on my mother as she was forced to play the double role of mom and dad.

When I was in second grade, my dad worked as an exterminator. On the job one day, he fell out of a roof and broke his back. He never regained his strength, status, or position as a man, an employee, or a provider. After the accident, my father never again worked a day in his life. This infuriated me. We went from a dual-income, middle-class family growing in success and prosperity to all of us living on my mom's grocery store salary. I hated my dad for not taking responsibility for us, for taking the easy way out, for giving in to his alcoholism, for allowing it to overcome him and ruin us. I found him lazy and pathetic. Who was I if my father was an unemployed, disabled alcoholic? One of the hardest conquests in life is overcoming our parents' limitations. If my dad amounted to nothing, how was ever going to be capable of anything more?

My anger was also fueled by who my father was in a drunken state. He was unpredictable and scary. Sometimes he was happy and cheerful. Most of the time, he yelled and screamed. It is enormously difficult as a child, craving—needing—stability, routine, comfort, to live with an alcoholic of this nature. It would have been more tolerable if my father was always mean and we knew to stay away from him when he was drinking. But sometimes, he was the best dad in the world—taking us out for ice cream and giving us piggyback rides as we walked down the street. I wanted him to be that dad all the time. As a little girl wanting her daddy's love and attention, I always took the risk and tried to get him to spend time with me, mostly getting the brunt of his anger. My presence alone would annoy him and he'd send me out of the room in tears after a hurtful comment. Watching television on Saturday morning was the most anxious time of my entire week. If the TV was too loud, my dad would come downstairs hollering and threatening us for waking him up. The frequency of his uncontrollable temper and unpredictable outbursts put us kids on edge growing up. My father was often embarrassing when drunk in public. One time at softball practice, he made a horrifying scene because my youngest brother had run into the woods to play and now that it was time to leave, we couldn't find him. My dad starts screaming his name, cursing, kicking the car tires, and banging his fists against the glass windows. I watched my softball team stare in shock at this violent man who was my father. The whispers and comments made me want to crawl into a hole and die right there.

At eleven years old, I ran away. I did it to make a point. I left a note, stating that I was never coming back to the house if my father was still there. I thought for sure this would get my mother's attention. She would definitely see how serious it was to be living with an active alcoholic. At 6:30 a.m., I left the house and walked to the nearby train station. I boarded the train at 6:45 a.m. and got off at 30th Street Station, a stop directly in Center City. It was a regular weekday morning and I was supposed to be in school. But I had an important mission. I needed to show my mom just how bad it was living with my dad. It didn't work out that way. My best friend was the only person who knew about my plan and also happened to be the first person my mother called when she found out I was missing. I was sitting on a bench in the train station in the middle of Philadelphia when my mom showed up. She did not appreciate my well thought out plan or the point I was trying to make. She was furious and I was forced to return home to live with the monster for another two years.

But God heard my cry. At thirteen, my father was arrested for forging prescriptions. My two brothers were in the car with him. That was all my mom needed. Once our safety was at risk, my mom took immediate action. He had to move out. When my mom came to my bedroom and told me Daddy was moving out in August, you would have thought she gave me a trip to Disney World. I was ecstatic, overjoyed. I literally jumped up and danced around my bedroom, hugging and kissing my mom. What a wonderful decision! Finally, freedom from the man I believed made my life miserable. With my father gone, I had choice in a relationship with him and I chose to no contact. For eight years, I did not see or speak to my father. But because resentments carry on a life of their own, I spent much time speaking of him. In my upcoming teenage years, there was plenty of opportunity for me to unleash my rage as I made my way through mental hospitals, eating disorder clinics, rehabs, therapists, psychiatrists. I had a view of my father as vicious and horrifying and I convinced plenty of others that he was a terrifying dad. Teachers, friend's parents, counselors, anyone who would listen to my sob story I told about the tragedies of my father: his screaming, unpredictability, drinking, rage, laziness, unemployment. Because of me, many, many people believed my dad to be a horrific, inhumane, violent alcoholic. If he were to go to shake their hand, having never met them before, he wouldn't stand a chance at being accepted because of the way I portrayed my dad to others. I gave people no chance to form their own opinion or make their own assessment of my father's character. I withheld the possibility of a tremendous amount of love being offered to my dad by ensuring that everyone knew of his terribleness as a father, a man, a human being. The impact of my cruelty hit me with an overwhelming shock: I was playing God.

Who am I to determine how much love a person is to receive? *Who am I* to decide what is forgivable? Preparing you for who my father was before you had an opportunity to experience him yourself, guaranteed that you would judge and resent him exactly as I did, thereby limiting all possibility of goodness towards him. *Who am I* to inhibit God's grace and mercy? Forgiveness came not from accepting who my father was, but from seeing how my perception of him had been wrong.

In the light of my own recovery and personal experience with addiction, I was suddenly able to see my part in our tumultuous relationship. I had not made life easy on him either. I was constantly nagging on him for smoking, for having a beer in his hand. I tried to make him feel guilty, bad, and wrong every day for being what I termed a "loser dad." My image of "father" was not who my dad was and herein lies the incongruence. The freedom of forgiveness came when I took the burden of "daddy" off my father. I no longer made him responsible for meeting my unrealistic expectations. I no longer demanded he fulfill my every outrageous need. I stopped relying on him to be the source of my emotional stability. I set my father free to be exactly who he is and is not. I allowed him to be all that he can, all that he is, and all that he wasn't, and all that he'll never be. I gave my father permission to be just another human being.

The greatest error in my perception was that I associated my anger with my father. I hated *him*. Not the disease of alcoholism, not the depression, not the behaviors, not the neglect nor the hurt. I hated my *dad*—as a person, as a man, as a husband, and especially as a father. Therein lies my harm: identifying *him* as the problem. The truth is, my father was a delightful man, quite charming with the ladies, sociable and outgoing in the community. He knew how to read a map better than a truck driver and was a flower enthusiast. He could talk on any sport with the knowledge and accuracy of a broadcaster. His general disposition was confident, powerful, and welcoming. The fact that I never saw this began to pain me deeply. I started to realize that my resentment was blocking me from enjoying who my father truly was: a great and brilliant man.

Months later, after having made a beautiful amends with my father over dinner at his favorite restaurant, I was in the throes of a devastating bulimic episode. Crying on my hands and knees by the toilet, I reached up for my cell phone to call my dad. I wanted to hear his voice. I wanted to know he loved me. When my dad answered the phone, I told him that bulimia was killing me. I said that I didn't know how it was going to end and that I was scared. My father's response healed any vestigial of hurt that still existed from my childhood. He stopped everything and said, "Sara, I'm coming to get you." Within ten minutes, I was in a car driving to a diner with my dad where we sat for ninety minutes. For the first time in my life, I allowed myself to be comforted and loved by a father who recognized his child's pain. I was honest and vulnerable and he was warm and compassionate. He told me witty jokes to make me smile and pushed my hair out of my tear-streaked cheeks. He understood not a thing about eating disorders, but he heard the cry of despair in my heart. He asked what he could do to help me and told me I was beautiful. If I ever had a hole in my heart just for my daddy, he filled it that night.

Step Nine: We made direct amends to such people wherever possible, except when to do so would injure them or others.

Once I had my list and had become willing, the next step involves the actual making of amends, which means righting of a wrong. True learning implies a permanent change of behavior. If I have truly incorporated the principles of the previous eight steps into my everyday existence, by now I am a very different person. By making amends, I face the people I have wronged, state truthfully my past behaviors and sincerely ask for forgiveness. What can I do to make this right? Financial amends were simplistic: I pay back the money I stole plus more. But the others, I was scared. Afraid of what other people would think of me when I exposed how I had hurt them. Afraid of other's reactions when I disclosed what I had done. By tackling the easy ones first, I gained faith that I would not crumble in embarrassment when it came time for the huge ones. When completing a conversation, I began to ask the question, "Is there anything that I have not included that upsets you about me in any way?" I would further state, "Please be reassured that I would like to correct any and all disturbance between us, leaving nothing incomplete." I requested free and open communication with no fear of anything being taken personal.

This had a profound and enormous effect on both me and the person with whom I would be speaking. The ninth step stopped being about me feeling better and started to become about the other person's healing. It creates the space for a person, once traumatized by my behavior, to express without fear the pain and upset I had brought to their lives, their heart, and their families. I listened, calmly, compassionately, sincerely. By validating the horror of someone's experience, it makes it okay for them. I found myself begging my brother to allow me to somehow make up for robbing him of his collection of bicentennial quarters. I had forgotten about that but it became clear when I asked him if there was anything else, he had not. As a little boy, my brother collected those quarters for almost a decade. They were his treasure, his hobby, his thrill. In my active addiction, in the coldness of cocaine, I stole his entire collection. He was only twelve years old.

The miracle of the ninth step lies in a unified connection, when I can get into the world of another human being. My brother was devastated over that incident. Even more was that he hated himself for being angry with me. Joe had the ability to separate his sister from her addiction. He knew I was not performing those acts of injustice, he knew it was drugs controlling me. Joe loved me so much that he was upset with himself because he blamed me and not my addiction. With every other incident, Joe was able to forgive me but not with the quarters. He had so much of his heart in that collection, that I had taken a part of him when I had taken those quarters. Years of patience and persistency, commitment and focus went into building his collection. His pain was not in the loss of the financial value, although that was very real. The crushing blow came on a young boy who experienced his first taste of betrayal at my hands. My stealing his quarters symbolized the destruction of his hopes and dreams, the ruin of his hard work and intense effort. He was only twelve years old. It hurt my soul that I did not even remember this incident when I went to make an amends to him. I sobbed and he held me, telling me it's okay now. It's really okay. And in his arms, I knew that he was talking about himself. In my attempt to make peace with my past, my brother had healed.

There was one relationship in which I was uncertain as to how to make amends. This was my daughter. Laila was two years old when I had gotten clean and I spent a lot of her infancy in rehabs or running the streets in addiction. Through the fourth step, I had cleared the shame of not knowing who her father was. I no longer felt dirty or inadequate because I had slept with more than one man the month I had gotten pregnant. But there was still a gnawing feeling around what that meant for Laila.

After two false paternity tests within three months of Laila's birth, I decided to write the names of the others on a piece of paper and store it away until she was older. I rationalized that if she wanted to find out who her father was when she was eighteen, I would give her the list and she could do so. I attempted to justify this in my head but the truth is always clear in my heart. It is not a child's responsibility to identify their parents. I decided as my amends to Laila that I would find out who her dad was.

This proved to be a daunting task for numerous reasons. Namely, I was over five years clean and Laila was now seven years old. It had been eight years since I had contact with any of the possible fathers. My addiction did not include relationships. My promiscuity involved numerous one-night stands with most of the guys I used cocaine with. I did not know where most of them lived and did not even have last names for some. Getting ahold of any of the men in question seemed impossible and even dangerous for me. And it was. However, it was unnecessary for me to fear. The beauty of the eighth step is that it releases a spirit of willingness into the energy of the universe which brings forth the opportunity for the ninth step. I did not have to seek anyone out specifically or tangibly. I did not have to reenter the drug culture to locate these men. I did not have to return to old hangouts and ask around for their whereabouts. Instead, I prayed nightly for God to provide me a way to find Laila's dad. And the miracles began...

Within a week of placing my intention into the universe, unbelievable occurrences starting happening. People were brought back into my path that I had not even run into at a mall in over eight years. Guys I had not even passed by on the road showed up in my world again. By staying close to God through prayer, I was prepared when God indicated it was time for me to act.

I was with my home group members at the diner that we attended regularly after my Monday night meeting. To my absolute astonishment, in walked one of the candidates! I immediately turned to my recovery friends sitting at the table with me. I needed support, encouragement, and direction—I was freaking out with internal anxiety. It all felt surreal. I didn't feel ready but I knew I had to speak to him before one of us left this diner. After some coaching and reassurance, I walked into the bathroom to pray. My plan was to pass by his table and request to speak with him. In the stall, I gave the entire situation to God through a third-step affirmation. I prayed intently. I had no idea how to approach him or what to say if he agreed to speak with me. I was scared because he was sitting with a girl who, from a bystanders viewpoint, appeared to be his girlfriend. I did not want to embarrass him, offend her, or cause any further harm. Praying for courage, I took a final deep breath and stepped out of the bathroom. There he stood, in front of me, waiting for me. I looked into his eyes to say hello and I knew: he knew. He had followed me into the restroom for the same reason I had gone in—to build up my strength to ask him that question: will you take a paternity test? We both needed to find out. We exchanged numbers and soon scheduled the testing.

He turned out *not* to be Laila's dad. His years of wonder, worry, and curiosity were relieved and I started back at square one with a new faith. I renewed my prayer request and this time, waited in anticipation for the universe to bring the next possibility into my life.

A few weeks later, divine intervention again revealed itself. I stopped at a service station in my neighborhood where I rarely ever go to for gas. It was a known hangout for drug deals and I spent much time there in my using days so I avoided it now in recovery. I don't know why it even occurred to me to stop there aside from spiritual impulse. As I was handing money to the cashier, Will walked into the store. Now a twenty-four-year-old woman, I had not seen him since I was sixteen. Our eyes met and instantly, as if reading each other's minds, we both knew we were thinking the same thing: it's time to find out the truth.

Will walked over to me, squarely and confidently and immediately told me that he was my daughter's father. He said that he has known in his heart since the day I got pregnant and has thought about her every day since. I will state that Will had a fifty-fifty chance of correctly guessing the moment of inception being that we only had sex twice. I'll also note that Laila was now seven years old and we still lived in the exact same house in Croydon, leaving Will ample opportunity to contact us. Circumstances aside, it was perfect in God's time. I would not have been prepared nor even slightly open to identifying Laila's dad one day prior to my ninth step.

It turns out Will is Laila's father. He was still active in the drug life, addicted to heroin and returning to jail frequently. Being caught up in addiction, Will did not pursue nor push to be an active father in Laila's life and I was thankful for that. I was unwilling to allow him any degree of involvement with her. My intention was not to provide a father figure for my child. My amends was complete. I had a name for Laila.

In the years to come, Laila and I would talk about her dad, how we met and why I choose not to let him around her at the time. A few years later, Will wrote a letter to Laila. He was clean ten months and had another baby on the way. After days of prayer and much discussion, Laila met her dad for the first time at the Neshaminy State Park on Easter weekend of 2008. She was ten years old.

Step Ten: We continued to take personal inventory and when we were wrong promptly admitted it.

This step offers an invaluable tool which can prevent me from backsliding into the dark and devastating path of self-destruction. Isolation leads me to dishonesty, and vice versa. Both will ultimately end in self-hatred, guilt, and remorse. Through a daily ten-step inventory, I am unable to refuse to acknowledge my mistakes and thereby seek to secretly hide them away. Every night, I wrote a mini-inventory. Sometimes it looked like bullet points, other times it was extensive writing. Sometimes I mentally reviewed my day. For me, a long-term mental review is insufficient. I begin to lie to myself, keeping secrets, and harboring repressed anger and unacknowledged feelings. Pent-up frustration is never useful for me as I have a difficult time coping with anger. When I fully feel the anger burning within, I want to commit either homicide or suicide but at best, I'll settle for massive self-destruction. I don't know what to do with the feeling, how to allow it to pass, or the ways in which to comfort myself when I am experiencing it. The tenth step catches my upset before it can lead to further harm of myself or another person. It is a daily review of steps four through nine where I honestly look at my errors, tell another person about it, and make corrections where applicable.

In the AA Big Book, Bill Wilson refers to anger as a luxury of more balanced people and not a feeling an alcoholic can afford to dwell in. He even goes as far as to state that resentment is the number one difficulty in maintaining sobriety. I had to develop a working mechanism for the processing and elimination of my anger that did not include bulimia.

Here are some of the points I would consider in my nightly tenth step:

- Is there any part of the day where I am uncomfortable about what occurred, what was said, how a situation transpired, another's reaction, etc.?
- Had my thoughts, feelings, words, and actions throughout the day reflected my truest values?
- I looked at what I had done well and what could use improvement. Did I set goals for the day and meet them?
- Was I living up to my potential in every area of my life? As a woman, mother, friend, sister, employee, etc.?
- I wrote what I had left undone and what I was afraid to say.
- I included what was helpful and what caused discord.
- Where was God in my day?
- Where was a newcomer in my day?
- How and where and in what way did I assist another human being?

- Is there anything I need to make amends for today?

Part of my tenth step included sitting quietly for ten minutes prior to writing in order to gain a centered perspective in preparation for my daily review. I could be more honest and accurate if I was not anxious and scattered. This was great practice for the upcoming eleventh step. In this time of silent attention, I would contemplate all that had occurred throughout the day. I began to make use of this in the morning as well. Some of my morning thoughts focused on the following topics:

- What is my intention for the day?
- Is there anything I am scared about, excited for, or anticipating today?
- Do I have any concrete goals to work toward today and what are they?
- Who will I reach out to in time of need today?
- Who will I offer support to today?
- Is there anything left over from yesterday that I need to clean up today?
- What didn't align with principles yesterday that I can I do differently today?
- Where will God be in my day?

If these morning and evening questions seem dauntingly overwhelming, it may be that I need to develop the discipline and commitment necessary to attain excellence. This step keeps me on track with God's will for me by correcting my errors promptly, thereby removing the interference of self-will. Over time, these questions became engrained in who I am. By following the guiding principles of honesty and responsibility, it became possible for me to be the best person I can be in all areas of my day. I began to think before reacting as these points would often come to mind as I went about my daily activities. Like a gentle, loving influence, the tenth step—this continual self-reflection—began to steer my life in a uniquely purposeful way. I had direction in life and a standard for life. I developed realistic expectations and formulated workable goals. The code of conduct the tenth step introduced me to freed me to live in accordance with my highest ideals without being bogged down by the burden of secrecy.

Step Eleven: We sought through prayer and meditation to improve our conscious contact with God as we understood Him, praying only for knowledge of His will for us and the power to carry that out.

The first three steps helped me to realize the nature of my disease and introduced me to the solution of the program. Steps four through seven helped me to realize the nature of myself and allowed me to gain acceptance with who I am. Steps eight and nine helped me to realize the nature of relationships and placed me on proper terms with others. Step ten helps me to maintain this newfound balance and serenity. I am now ready to learn more about the nature of God.

I had grown up in a religious family. We attended mass every Sunday (one of the three rules of the house, the other two being dinner at Grandmom's at 5:15 p.m. every night and no boys in the bedrooms), I spent twelve years in Catholic school, and we said bedtime prayers as a family every night. I didn't have horror stories regarding abusive nuns at school or priests at church. Growing up, we were taught to give everything to God. I found God to be warm, loving, and forgiving. I had sought God since I was little, always having an inherent longing to be near and close to God's presence. I prayed for God's direction in most everything I did. God was simply always on my mind from as young as I can remember thinking. In my desire to know God, prayer was consistent for me. It was my comfort and greatest companion.

While on my sixth step, emotional and unmanageable as I came face-to-face with my deepest defects of hopeless terror and self-hatred, my sponsor suggested I begin meditating to calm the insanity of my thoughts. I was not unfamiliar with the practice of meditation. I had begun to sit quietly with guided audio tapes by Deepak Chopra and Wayne Dyer back when I was fifteen. It was then that I started studying spiritual leaders such as Louise Hay, Brian Weiss, and Gary

Zuvac. I enjoyed the spiritual journey, actually, I craved it. I knew it as my source of fulfillment but something always was more attractive and alluring than God so I remained in a constant state of turbulence and eternal dissatisfaction.

Now that I had arrived at the eleventh step, it was time for me to once again sit still. Coming into recovery and getting clean, this was not yet a natural or comfortable place for me to be. In fact, I could accurately describe some sittings as excruciatingly painful, agonizing even. I could sit for a little under ten minutes until I could no longer be still. I had to move. I had to get out of my skin. I had to focus on something else. I had to jump. I had to run because I did not yet feel worthy of God's love nor did I value myself enough yet to nurture self-care.

It is said that prayer is talking to God and meditation is listening for God's response. I had always been the talker. Praying incessantly for God to help, fix, save, cure, rescue me from some self-imposed tragedy. Yet I had never listened. I had not practiced waiting long enough to hear God speak. This was the most precious, vital, and important piece of the eleventh step for me and continues to remain so today. I can spend hours and years of my life submitting prayer requests before God and in God's incomprehensible grace and mercy, He provides for me despite my ingratitude. When have I asked God what He wanted from me? I didn't ask that question because my soul knew the answer: God wanted *all* of me. Not some areas of my life, not just the pain, not only at weddings and funerals, not a few selected defects. God wants *all* of me: my joy and dreams, lies and tears, self-destruction and hopelessness, relationships and solitude, money and driving. God wants *all* of me. And when I sat still in the quiet silence with God, I had to face that I was cutting God out from numerous areas of my life. Self-will still permeated my family relationships, financial matters, bulimia recovery. I had to learn to sit with God through all of my success and mistakes, accepting uncon-ditional love regardless. It is not an easy task when first learning to meditate in recovery to sit and stay with God before you experience God. It requires the trust from the third step to believe that when we call, God hears and is there with us. It requires persistent commitment and patience as we build our channel of communication. The best I could do some days was simply not give up. If I could spend only four minutes in meditation that morning, then that is what I could do. Sometimes I could manage twenty minutes. Most days I could tolerate ten. It was a learning experience and like any other skill, got better in time with practice.

I renewed my spiritual quest that I had embarked upon at fifteen, committing myself to an inner journey to discover truth. I began studying Eastern religions, went on spiritual retreats, attended many workshops and functions, took all my college electives in philosophy and theology, and poured over ancient texts. I've read the Bible, Upanishads, and Bhagavad Gita as I immersed myself in esoteric studies. I searched for the answer to the ultimate problem of me. I looked everywhere for God other than exactly where I was. In my pursuit for wholeness, it took me years to realize that I had never been broken.

As I continued in my spiritual study, meditation became a regular and necessary part of my life. Like any other habit we develop, we have to be committed, persistent, and consistent. What had seemed impossible initially soon became an easy and fulfilling practice. I could often sit for twenty or more minutes twice a day without that being intolerable.

Then one day, without warning or cause, a remarkable transformation occurred. I don't know why and I don't know how but I realized one day that I honestly craved stillness. I had come to know God in the quietness and I yearned for Him. Throughout the months and years of initial meditation, there were definite phases I passed through. As I reflect on the stages of coming to know God, everything was in its perfect order.

In the beginning, the quiet was uncomfortable. Then it became just silence as the internal dialogue of my mind began to cease. The less I paid attention to it, the weaker the thoughts became. From silence, I found a sense of peace. I was only able to identify and recognize it as peace because it was different from anything I had ever known. It came with a deep, intuitive sense that everything was going to be all right. Following peace, I discovered bliss. This was a state of joyous ecstasy that I begged God not to let me leave. I consider it being in the presence of angels and describe it as singing to God. As the bliss passed, I entered into a state of nothingness so complete that I could hear God. My personal process was my own unique journey from which I came to know without a doubt: God is.

My experience of prayer consisted of a variety of forms. Coming from a Catholic upbringing, I often incorporated childhood prayers in my daily time with God. I also prayed the rosary on a regular basis and read from a few special prayer books. Those are formal prayers for me. Informal prayer is ongoing and unceasing. It's me talking with God, inviting Him into the moment, bringing God into my awareness. I'd speak to God like I would to a friend that I was getting to know. I'd share my day with God—my hopes, activities, regrets. Anger, happiness, joy, and sorrow were all discussed in conversations with God. I'd submit my requests, express my heart's desires, and evaluate my dreams.

Daily I'd ask for knowledge of God's will for me and the power to carry it out. Throughout the day, I'd check in with God, especially when I had to make a decision, needed to have a difficult conversation, or was facing a tough task. It became a habit for me to ask for God's guidance and direction prior to taking any action. It became remarkably clear that when I was living in the flow of God's will, life happened naturally, smoothly, and peacefully. Then I began to desire God's will more than my own. This was a process of maturation. I saw how when I went against God's order, I suffered. As a result of continuous pain, I realized that God's plan was the best plan and I was willing to give up more and more of my stubborn drives. Then, the most profound shift occurred: I suddenly realized that God's will had become my will. I wanted what God wanted for me. I had a relationship with God that was built on trust and experience. By consistently dedicating time to spend in God's presence, I became a channel for God to express His glory and greatness. My only purpose was to be an instrument of creation for God. I'd offer myself to God each day and ask to be a vehicle of His love. To have the privilege of carrying a message for God is an unspeakable honor.

Along with this shift in consciousness came innumerable gifts. God was changing my thoughts and intentions and placing extraordinary desires on my heart. There appeared an amazing willingness previously unknown, and I could easily let go of anything once God revealed it to be so. All I wanted was to do God's will, whatever that may be for my life, my day, my world. I began to develop a gentle peace and compassionate disposition. The fulfillment I sought as a teenager was alive and real in me. But this time, there was nothing calling me from experiencing it. And as much as I know that today is Monday, I know that I will always be abundantly provided for when I rest in God's care.

Since my first eleventh step, my relationship and understanding of God has grown, developed, diminished, shattered, and been rebuilt on a foundation of truth. Today, honesty pervades every aspect of the intimacy I share with God. I stand before God open and exposed, submitting my entire being to Him. There is nothing I withhold from God today. I keep no secrets hidden. A solemn, devotional love of God drives my every moment. I remain in constant communion with my Creator through prayer and meditation.

- Prayer: speaking to God; offering my everything to God
- Meditation: silent stillness where I listen and commune with God

I still believe strongly that God wants to know my personal requests and that He desires to fulfill the petitions of my heart. God still frequently listens to my burdensome regrets and remorseful complaints and even when I don't "feel" God, I know God is there. My spiritual belief allows me to participate in a co-creator relationship with God, provided I know my role as an avenue of expression. In that partnership, making my wants, hopes, and dreams known to God is a vital component and the first tool of the eleventh step. Listening to God's response is the second piece.

Step Twelve: Having had a spiritual awakening as a result of these steps, we tried to carry this message to addicts and to practice these principles in all our affairs.

The twelfth step contains three keys components: spiritual awakening, carrying the message, and principles in all affairs. My personal understanding of a spiritual awakening is the impossible becoming possible. There was a time in my life when staying clean was not an option. I could not do it no matter what I tried. With the help of the NA program, I had remained clean and drug-free for many years. That alone is nothing short of an incomprehensible and unexpected miracle. Family relationships that were more like a war zone had transformed into an enjoyable experience of companionship. That was not only unlikely, it was virtually impossible because of all the devastation and anger resulting from my addiction. These amazing twelve steps allowed me to enter into the realm of the Spirit where the miraculous occurs. This spiritual awakening is included as part of the twelve step process, it is not a side effect, by-product, reward, or payoff. It is not something that happens only for a random few. It is actually one of the twelve steps. If I was to remain clean and in recovery, I was going to experience a spiritual awakening as a result of working through the steps.

The second component is carrying the message. A key principle of recovery is generosity: I keep what I have only by giving it away. It is my duty, honor, privilege, and responsibility to help others the way I was helped. People became my friends, welcomed me into their homes, invited me to events, asked how I was doing, called to check in with me, developed relationships with my family. The people of NA taught me friendship, support, and love. One of my jobs as a recovering woman is to reach out to the newcomers and ensure they are welcomed, supported, and encouraged.

I had a sponsor who guided me through the twelve steps. This is the central way we give back because the steps are the foundation of our recovery. As an experienced member of NA who has been through all twelve steps, I need to be available to take others through the steps. It is our way to God, our path to personal freedom, the entire solution of our twelve-step program. The most useful tool I can give to another person in recovery is an understanding and experience of the steps.

I spent time in rehabs and institutions and there were always meetings. This is part of carrying the message. Taking the commitments into the facilities. Showing the hopeless detoxing addict that we can and do stay clean. Sending a message of hope to the girl who wants to die. This is a great and valuable form of NA service.

There are innumerable ways we can carry the message: the NA newsletter, service commitments, holding positions on a committee, sharing freely and openly with the addict in the workplace who has a problem, reaching out to the neighbor's daughter after her mother asks us to talk with her, speaking at meetings and conventions, showing up and participating in the fellowship. Everyone has unique and individual talents, skill sets, and preferences. These differences allow us to help a diverse group of people. Personal recovery is not a one-size-fits-all. Your fourth and seventh steps are not going to be identical to my fourth and seventh step experiences. Recovery is big enough to encompass all and include everyone. Service work is the same. There is a brand and a fit for anyone. The important thing is that you are giving back.

The final piece of step 12 is practicing these principles in all of our affairs. This is where I ran into a problem: in every area of my life, spiritual principles had to dominate. God had to be allowed to operate in all aspects of my world and I had to be willing to give up self-will in everything I was involved in.

Due to recovery, my world had blossomed. I was no longer useless, worthless, broke, lost, helpless, or dysfunctional. I now had family relations, parenting, employment, finances, friendships, education, and personal recovery. Areas of my life included community and neighborhood, family and motherhood, ministry and college, career and home life, romance and hobbies. I was a whole person with a real life managing real-world responsibilities! This step declares that I must adhere to the newfound spiritual principles such as honesty, integrity, faith, tolerance, love, kindness, peace, and usefulness in each and every area of my life. All of it. Nothing can be

held back from inclusion or the foundation of my recovery is insecure. Dishonesty cannot be acceptable in my work place without also
eventually appearing in my relationships. Hypocrisy is a dangerous
game and I learned later on that it's potentially lethal.

The final part of step 12 requires that I practice what I preach.
Sharing clean in meetings while living inappropriately in other ways
is intolerable to my spirit. The incongruence between who I pretend
to be for you and who I know I am inside traps me in a violent façade
of isolation and despair. I feel fraudulent because I am. The truth will
be exposed in the end and I may be backed so far into a corner by
then that the only coping skill I know to use at that time is getting
high.

That is why honesty is an integral component throughout the
entire twelve steps. Secrets keep us sick. What I am hiding from you
I am hating myself for. And when I hate myself, I seek to destroy
myself. It is said that there are three invaluable facets of the program:
the "how" it works:

- Honesty: telling the truth about my feelings, thoughts,
  actions—entirely and completely
- Open-mindedness: listening for a solution other than my
  own; taking suggestions
- Willingness: ready and able to take action different than I
  have done in the past; to change

Without all three of these factors playing leading roles in my
daily living, recovery will be off-balanced. Narcotics Anonymous is
a twelve-step program and the foundational principles for each and
every one of the steps are honesty, open-mindedness, and willingness. When I do not consistently and actively apply these principles
in my life and personal recovery, I veer off track and head down a
path of regression. Sometimes with devastating effects.

Major Transitions

As with every ordinary person's life, my recovery was marked by multiple defining moments. At these times, my response triggered a ripple effect which would set a course for years to come. Some decisions proved to be quite tragic, others profoundly beneficial. All in all, certain events charted the path which has led me to the present.

College

The first of these times was my decision to return to college. Through the steps, I had uncovered within myself a passion for learning. The fourth through seventh steps is a remarkable process of purification as it removes the filth from the lens from which I view the world. Now seeing rightly and clearly, I was able to identify parts of myself that had never before been acknowledged. For me, I found a deep desire to obtain knowledge and longed to absorb new information. I had awakened my heart's calling to study and master vast fields of academia—particularly in the unseen and abstract worlds. However, as I went through classes, every subject intrigued me and I found myself captivated by each course. From theology and philosophy to American literature and economics, it all fascinated me. I found myself relating and integrating all forms of information. Yoga and psychology, neurobiology and anthropology—all of it had my undivided interest. I was in awe by this world of unlimited knowledge and resources. I quickly became enamored with my studies. I knew in the deepest part of me, as my soul yearned with a familiar recognition, that education and learning was my fulfillment.

For the first time, I saw how my recovery was changing and effecting and building my entire life. I was using the same tools for success in the classroom as I using for success in recovery. In school, I sat up front and raised my hand, exactly as I had been taught at meetings. I participated by making comments and asking questions, allowing the teachers and others to get to know me, exactly the things that had helped me stay connected in early recovery. I reached out for help when I was confused about the material, as I had learned to do by working steps with a sponsor. The skills I was demonstrating in the classroom parallel to the healthy tools of a recovery program. Throughout my college career, continued interaction with professors and peers helped me to build lifelong mentors and friendships. After class, I would read through the materials I had just learned and take notes on important concepts. I had done this in early recovery as I read through program literature and then would write my thoughts, feelings, and insights in my journal. I showed up at class early and stayed after it ended, for exclusive time with the instructors. All these tools—the keys to successfully navigating college—I had learned and developed in NA! Recovery was more than just not using drugs—it filtered through my entire world and had become a way of life.

About a year into my return to college, I faced another important turning point. Its effects were to color many years to come. It involves a deeply painful heartbreak. I had briefly dated an NA friend about a year prior. It was short-lived but impactful. With my new-found spiritual and emotional freedom, I hadn't wanted to be tied down to a relationship at the time. I wanted to focus on my dreams and desires. My attention was on building my education and growing intellectually. I had always been around males to fill a codependent need in my heart. Male sexual attention was the foundation of my self-esteem and sole source of identity. However, through step work, this false sense of self had been magically transformed. There was no longer an insatiable need to have a man filling an emotional void within me. I felt confident in my own being. I wanted to be with me because I was somebody special and I knew that. And I honored that. Finally, at peace with who I was without any need to obtain approval from anyone outside of myself.

Released from my childhood chains of emotional deficiency, I was free to decide who I wanted to be with, to date, or to spend time with. I was charting unknown territory. I viewed the world before me as a blank canvas: anything was possible. In this exalted state, I faced life with enthusiasm and wanted nothing to hinder my personal adventure of creation. Alex was an excellent man, truly a kind soul. He genuinely loved me and was sincere in his words and gentleness toward me. He was soft and romantic, intelligent, and worldly. But I wanted my freedom. The world was opening up before my very eyes and I was mesmerized by the wonder of it all. I ended our relationship the week I returned to college. He was devastated and heartbroken while I was free and unencumbered.

Heartbreak

A year later, I had grown comfortable in my new situation and life once again felt balanced and stable. I was still active in NA—with sponsorship, meetings, step work, and service. I had friends that I spent time socializing with, often bringing along my daughter. We travelled to the zoo, spent two summers enjoying Tuesdays in Wildwood, visited museums in the city, packed lunches for picnics in the parks, and went camping with other recovering people. My daughter could roller skate and ski before she was five because they were our common hobbies. I was waitressing part-time which gave me sufficient funds for what I needed. And there was school, which generated such fulfillment and purpose in my life that everything else worked.

One of the best decisions I had ever made, possible the single only positive decision I had made up to that point in my life, was returning to college. I discovered that I love to learn. In fact, I lived for knowledge. I realized unknown, hidden passion and dreams by being a student. And I excelled at it—naturally and effortlessly. Studying was far from a bore, it was enthralling! I'd absorb class textbooks ahead of the teacher's syllabus and had the capacity to retain information at an alarming rate and depth. I often had weeks of homework done in advance.

This joy surrounding my life also carried with it a hint of loneliness. I was twenty-two years old and had been single for over a year. I desired a boyfriend. I began to long for the comfort, care, and companionship shown to me by Alex, my ex-boyfriend. In my pursuit for independence, I had ended the relationship. Yet now, I wanted to return. I took a week in prayer and meditation and intensive analysis with my sponsor. I was ready but scared so I asked God to send me a sign indicating that it was okay to proceed with contacting Alex. There was a song Alex and I had danced to at a wedding reception we attended together. The song was beautiful and symbolized our intimacy. It's rarely played on the radio and not common to hear in ordinary music. It was special for us as a couple. So I made a deal with God: if I heard that song in the next ten days, I would know that God wanted me to move forward in reconnecting with Alex.

Eight days later, I was walking through the Oxford Valley mall and I heard it, Shakira's song "Underneath Your Clothes." I had never even noticed that the mall played surround sound music. I squeezed the hand of my girlfriend who was with me and I skipped down the center of the mall. Literally skipping and jumping and exuberant. God said yes! I asked for God's approval, waited until God indicated the time was right, and here it was! I was given permission to contact Alex and tell him what I had been yearning to say: I missed him and I had never stopped loving him and I wanted to give us another chance.

I went home that evening and called Alex. I left a message. A few nights later, while at work at the diner, I got a text message. It read, "I miss you too." It was Alex. My heart exploded and I could barely contain the joy that arose within me. We soon ended up reuniting and rekindled our love. For the first time in my entire life, I let go completely. Alex had my heart, soul, mind, and being. I gave him all of me in full trust and sincerity. If Alex would have asked me to marry him, I would have said yes without flinching. And this was a state I had not ever experienced before, being fully committed to a man and seeing a vision of our future.

Instead of planning our lives together, shortly after reestablishing our relationship, Alex decided it wasn't right for him. His words were one of those moments where time stands still. I was driving down the highway with my daughter and we had pulled into the McDonald's parking lot about to enter and buy her an ice cream cone. Alex told me he had to talk with me. He said, "Sara, you're a great girl and you're going to meet a really great guy. But it's not me."

Total devastation comes semi-close to the feeling I experienced. During impactful moments, people often remember odd and specific details regarding the event. I was wearing blue jeans and a purple jacket. I had white sneakers on that were slightly dirty and I had thought earlier that morning that I needed to buy a new pair. The car I was driving was my baby blue Saturn and Laila's gray booster seat was behind the passenger side because I liked to look at her smile as I drove. It was a Saturday afternoon and Alex and I had plans to go hear a band play at a local coffee house that evening.

My knees buckled and I almost dropped to the concrete in the parking lot of McDonald's. Whatever vital life force holds us together, left me at that moment. The yogis call it kundalini; the Chinese call it chi. In Hinduism, it's referred to as prana. Whatever philosophy I mold my energetic beliefs into, I literally felt it shoot down through my spine and leave out my body. I was shattered. My vision blurred as I held back tears. I wouldn't realize it until years later, but it was at this moment that I lost the energy to love.

Anorexia

For six weeks following that conversation with Alex, I lived in a state of complete numbness. I exercised compulsively and ate sparingly. It rapidly progressed to extreme levels. Four hours of cardio minimum daily, four hundred calories maximum a day. I had to control the out of control feelings. I had to control something, anything, everything, so I chose all of the above. Anorexia allowed me to be a high achiever and super accomplished through rigidity and relentlessness. I became a cold, harsh, and isolated individual. I was not a person, not a human, not a woman. I walked around as a shell in a lifeless robotic fashion. At the core of me, I am bulimic and this newly discovered ability to not eat thrilled me. I lost thirty pounds in a month and a half. When my weight would diminish to dangerous numbers, such as the mid to low '80s, I would increase my food plan by minuscule amounts, careful not to reactivate the bulimia but deathly afraid of malnourishment. Anorexia fueled my drive for success. I saw it as ambition, but in reality, it was distraction. I'd pay any cost to avoid the pain in me.

In a semi-unconscious and largely distorted effort to control the emotional devastation, I shut down and turned cold on the inside. For the next eight years, I did not allow a single person to come anywhere near me. I had no desire to love and no ability to cultivate it. In closing off one emotion, I inadvertently shut off all feeling. I often questioned and doubted my ability to love. I avoided dating and refused to allow my body to weigh above one hundred pounds. Love, like all spiritual principles, is all-encompassing in that I cannot pick and choose who I will love and who I won't. I either love or I do not. God either is or He isn't. I could not shut out the support from my friends in recovery without also blocking affection toward Laila. I could not be relentless with myself at the gym without also being harsh and unforgiving toward my mother. Love is not a pick and choose game. Like integrity, when I am out of love in one area of my life, it will trickle into every other area until a total takeover occurs and I am once again lost. Broken, cold, and alone. To avoid or control any of these feeling from arising within me, I resorted to eating disorder behaviors. Anorexia, bulimia, over-exercise, and weight became my barometers for esteem. It seemed better to distract myself with jean size and thigh measurements than to face and feel the horrid emptiness that had formed in my core. Obsession and compulsion returned and led to isolation which then established a terrible agony in my soul. In years to come, this process would prove disastrous as it depleted the foundation of my recovery.

Landmark

With six years clean, at the recommendation of a friend, I attended a weekend seminar in Philadelphia called Landmark Education. The reason this event is significant is because of the path it opened up before me. The teachings were based on reclaiming personal power by transcending all limitations and creating each moment anew. Landmark opens up the realm of possibility in any situation. Choice was the key concept. I took immediately to the seminar's curriculum. Freedom, empowerment, choice. I was attracted to the exhilaration generated in the atmosphere of Landmark. I compared it constantly to NA. Anorexia had me separated to a large degree mentally from the recovering addicts in meetings. I saw myself as different and dealing with an issue outside of recovery. I was looking for a way out. At the Landmark Forum seminar, the leader of the program discussed addiction and stated that support groups were unnecessary and served only to hold a person back by limiting what's possible in their recovery. I had yet to notice that Landmark itself requested commitments, service, active involvement, and further participation from its clients. The exact same supports that NA suggested and quite contradictory to the statements made by the Forum leader. We often hear only and exactly what we intend to hear. I wanted to way to make NA wrong and different, and I used Landmark to make that happen.

I grew more and more involved in Landmark, taking four seminars over a nine-month period. Major changes were occurring in my life both internally and externally. Inside, I was in constant conflict with what Landmark taught versus what I knew to be true for myself: I needed support. A group of like-minded individuals who share my common malady and encourage growth and recovery is greatly beneficial for me. In fact, it is what held me together and built me into a woman with dreams and a full life. Yet this "power and choice" message was persuasively attractive. I did not leave NA, but I did drastically cut down on meetings and involvement.

Eventually, I was offered a roommate situation with a Landmark friend. Laila and I could live there with minimal financial obligation while I completed my senior year of college. Laila was in second grade when we moved out to King of Prussia. It was forty-five minutes from my mother's house and my entire recovery community. I knew no one but the friend we were moving in with and was unfamiliar with the area. It was the first giant change I had made it recovery.

Laila started a new school, and I began attending new meetings. I committed to doing a thirty-in-thirty in my new area so I could build a foundation of support as I had in early recovery. I developed solid friendships both in NA meetings and the neighborhood. I picked a home group and cultivated a network. But it was difficult. I didn't choose a new sponsor in the area and was barely working with my former sponsor. I missed my old NA people and me and Laila seemed so far from everyone.

We stayed in King of Prussia with a roommate for nine months. Laila completed the second grade, and I graduated with my bachelor's degree. I told Laila she could pick any vacation spot she wanted to celebrate my achievement and we went to Disney World. It was an exciting trip that bonded us as mother and daughter. Florida was the perfect culmination to our strenuous effort over the previous year. It had not been easy on either one of us. I was tense, burdened, and constantly "busy" with the stress of senior thesis, Landmark commitments, change, and building a new recovery foundation. At seven years old, Laila was anxious, afraid, and often on her own. She was a latch key girl since second grade and knew to lock the door behind her, prepare a snack, and do her homework. We had made it through a scary transition, both doing the best we knew how to, and the trip to Disney united us once again. It allowed us to get silly and play, let our worries go and have fun. After almost a year of pent up emotions, we ran around like carefree children in Disney World.

That summer, I was hired into my first college-level position as a case manager for a family service organization. I had predictable and sustainable income and we soon moved into our first real apartment. It was an exciting and adventurous time for me and Laila as we packed and unpacked, shopped on a budget, and I learned to pay bills and handle financial responsibility. The move required Laila to again change school and she began third grade with an entirely new different group of kids. For myself, I can move with ease but as a young child, the instability of moving made Laila anxious and uncomfortable. There were some very real perks about Abington though that made this transition easier.

First, we were only twenty minutes now from my mother's house, making contact more accessible and frequent. This offered great comfort and reassurance for Laila and provided family support for me. Also, we lived near the YMCA and became members of the community through exercise, swimming, gymnastics, and family events. The YMCA has always been a keystone in raising my daughter and building community in my life. We also lived on the same street as three of Laila's classmates. This was undoubtedly the saving grace that carried both Laila and myself through those four years in Abington. She is still close with her Parkview Ave girlfriends today and I still remain in contact with their parents. As a young, single mother, the support and love Abington offered was priceless and precious.

During this time, I was becoming more involved with Landmark courses and I found myself in a mental conundrum: power versus powerlessness. Although I still remained actively involved in both Landmark and Narcotics Anonymous for a long while, with this second move, I found myself further questioning NA's beliefs and teachings. I would attend NA in the area but did not fully commit nor involve myself to any degree. This slow but steady distancing would prove to be yet another naïve and disastrous decision.

MBA

With seven and a half years clean, I was still living in Abington with Laila, occasionally participating in NA but no longer working a solid program. We lived an active, full, enjoyable life together, me and my daughter. She had great neighborhood girlfriends and loved her new school. She got involved in the plays and did well in her studies. She was happy, growing, and blossoming in Abington. I could tell she finally felt secure and had a real sense of stability. And coming from a mother with a history of addiction and eating disorders, trust in life is a big deal.

I was assistant softball coach for Laila's fifth grade team and she was active in numerous sports. Her and her best friends shared Girl Scout trips, frequent sleepovers, and fun adventures together. We went bike riding and walking daily, particularly convenient that we lived three blocks from the Willow Grove Park, an extravagant shopping arena. Laila and I spent most of our weekend afternoons at the parks and playgrounds. We were always doing something that involved nature because we loved to be outdoors. It was a time of high prosperity for us. We travelled frequently, a passion we both share. Day trips to beaches were common, international cruises our top choice, and shore vacations carried sentimental value. We relished in planning and organizing our next trip.

About this time, I decided to return to college for an MBA degree. The local university offered a new, exciting twenty-month accelerated program specializing in international business. I applied, and after completing a few prerequisite courses, was accepted into Arcadia University's MBA program. Classes were held Wednesday nights from 5:00 to 10:00 p.m. To say the least, I loved it. The educational environment expanded my awareness and opened my world to include other like-minded individuals who were as driven and successful as myself. I excelled in the classroom and thoroughly enjoyed the learning experience. I was engaged, actively involved, and eagerly participating in the full structure of the MBA.

School work occupied much of my time and attention and I readily gave it my all. Now focused on the demands of the business degree and captivated by the company of others with similar intellectual pursuits, my attention to recovery rapidly diminished. Although a time of great material accomplishment and intellectual expansion, there was no balance as I had no close friends in recovery anymore and barely maintained any existing intimate relationships.

The MBA program was a major decision that had mixed consequences. On my hand, it rose me to a higher standard of living and learning. On the other hand, it was the distraction I needed to remove myself from recovery. I had a full and active life on the outside but no one was truly exposed to the real me on the inside: scared, lost, out of control, and lacking support. Sara without an active recovery program is broken and suicidal. In all outer appearances, I had it together, but a closer look would reveal that I was walking on shaky ground and soon would be falling apart.

Bulimia

The first crush I developed after years of noninterest in men was toward a fellow classmate in the MBA program. He was two or three years younger than me so I did not put forth much effort in pursuing a relationship. But he had my interest, attention, and curiosity. We shared many of the same hobbies—nature and being outdoors, academic achievements, travel and vacationing, and we were intellectual enthusiasts. Ideas, knowledge, and learning were common passions that inspired us both. He was one of the few people I've personally met in my life that could challenge and surpass me intellectually. (There are many people greatly more intelligent than I, however, I am speaking of those I've had interpersonal contact with.) He could think quicker, understand more thoroughly, debate stronger, access more accurately, articulate clearer, and absorb information more efficiently than I ever could. He had me beat in every area and this was an exciting challenge for me. He intrigued me tremendously. Being more advanced than me, I respected and admired him. I wanted to spend more time around him.

Our friendship easily developed and there was an obvious mutual attraction. I came to trust him. As our friendship grew, I opened my life up to Garrett. I began to share other parts of myself that I had been holding in for a very long time—my emotional nature. I disclosed my fears and worries, my anxieties and pain to him. I surprised even myself with the degree of vulnerability I was able to offer Garrett. I had long ago stopped revealing weakness to people. Yet I allowed him to truly get to know me: my thoughts, desires, dreams, fears, and past experience. Our conversations would last for hours and feel like ten minutes. I suddenly realized that I cared for Garrett on an emotional and meaningful level. It had been so long since I had bonded with another person. I trusted him, cared for him, admired him, was attracted to him, and respected him. These combined factors convinced me that he was boyfriend material, despite the age discrepancy. After nine months of being close friends, I honestly wanted more.

It was a few days after I admitted to myself that I wanted to be with Garrett that I planned to have a conversation with him where I shared my feelings and hopes of us developing a relationship. Then I received a phone call that would change my life and shatter my idealized image of Garrett. It was his girlfriend.

She knew of me and wanted me out of the picture. Garrett had been dating her for over two years and they had been living together for over a year. Although an on/off relationship, they were fully committed and loved each other. Since Garrett had failed to ever mention he was attached, his girlfriend filled me in on the details. She knew about our friendship and was warning me, with severe threats, to stay away from her man.

One time, Garrett and I sat on the bench at the mall and picked out partners for each other. Another time, we watched corny romantic movies and cataloged "Ideal Trait" lists for each other's future spouse. Often, we'd hold hands while climbing up the steep mountain trail behind the university. In Costa Rica, we got massages together in the cabana on the beachfront. No, there was never any contact of a sexual nature. But I had known this man privately and intimately for almost an entire year and it was all a façade.

He blatantly withheld vital information from me. In fact, we had discussed past relationships and future desires. He had led me to believe that he was an available man. And I believed him, fully, totally, and completely. Had I been aware that he had a girlfriend, one with whom he shared a residence, I would never have gotten so close. And maybe that was the lesson. I would not have ever opened up had I known the truth.

The betrayal rocked my world. I had been being deceived for over nine full months by someone who was very close to me. Needless to say, I was livid. Furious that I had trusted him so completely and enraged that he was lying the whole time. I was upset with myself that I had just decided, after a lengthy friendship, that I wanted a deeper relationship with him. I questioned how I could not have known, analyzed any signs I may have missed, berated myself for not seeing it sooner. A girlfriend! The whole time! That lived with him! I felt shattered inside. After years of self-sufficiency, I let myself open up and trust again. It felt as if the carpet was pulled right from under my feet and onto the floor I fell.

That weekend, I was scheduled to attend my annual OA retreat. It was here at this retreat that my relapse began. I was in a safe place, a position where I could process the upset and pain surrounded by friends in recovery. But I didn't. I didn't talk about the massive emotional crisis I had just experienced days before. I didn't mention the anger, disappointment, betrayal, loss, or aloneness that I felt seeping out of my pores. Instead, on the first morning after breakfast, I locked myself in the bathroom and threw up. It was the first time in over eight years that I had purged. Get these fucking feelings out of me. I returned to old coping skills and reactivated an addiction. I didn't care. My solution that day became bulimia.

Leaving NA

At eight years clean, I found myself relapsing into an eating disorder, unwilling to stop. Life quickly turned chaotic, destructive, and secretive. The disease had me. I was speaking for my eight-year anniversary at a meeting in Jenkintown when I began to believe the lie again. I convinced myself that I had nothing more to learn in NA. The program offered the twelve steps as the solution and I had gone through all twelve steps twice already. What else was there left for me?

That is where my crucial mistake occurred. The program is not just about me. Had I reviewed the twelfth step, I would have seen that carrying the message to others is a necessary part of the program. I had gotten better—a lot better. Because of the NA fellowship, I had a full and active life with lots of joy and success. Now it becomes my responsibility to stay and show the newcomers that it works. If everyone left NA when their lives improved, there would be no one left. This was my error: I only thought of myself. There was still an inherent selfishness that plagued my entire existence: every relationship, activity, every responsibility. I came first no matter what and my needs, wants, and desires held importance over everything and everyone else. Although this selfishness had improved through the years and the steps, it was never honestly removed or surrendered. So it was an obvious response that I would leave NA when it no longer held any "purpose" for me. The stubborn belief that it is the world's duty to serve my every whim and that I somehow have a "right" to pursue my interests at all costs and ahead of all else—is an erroneous misconception that I see developing into a grand scale societal issue. The relentless and self-righteous pursuit of personal pleasure, regardless of intention, has long-standing and dire consequences. This pattern of living breaks down relationships by making them unimportant—a secondary priority attended to only after the pressing "needs" of the individual are met. This mind-set is characteristic of the extent of my involvement with others throughout my entire life: family, friends, daughter, and community. They would have my time, attention, and focus only when and if, my higher, more important priorities were fulfilled. This total self-centeredness pervaded my entire being throughout my recovery, causing much suffering to myself and others, but making it that much easier to walk away when I decided to leave NA.

The twelfth step also requires principles in every area of my life. My relationship with my body and eating were major tenets of my recovery, but there is no love and tenderness in bulimia. I could not claim unconditional tolerance as I deathly feared my weight rising above one hundred pounds. I could not practice generosity while stuffing my face with unnecessary food that I was wasting during a binge. There is no kindness during the violent act of purging. Resorting back to old behaviors without being honest about my actions is a dangerous and risky endeavor. Because of my clean time, of having been through the steps, of my experience in recovery, because of the fear of judgment, but more accurately, because I did not want to stop—I choose to leave NA instead of discussing the issue with my recovering friends. No one knew about the severity of my problem. No one knew how rapidly I fell into desperate levels of despair. No one knew how my disease corrupted my thinking. No one knew what I was going through.

I could no longer share recovery in a meeting while being at home with my head in the toilet. As bulimia took over, I was lying, stealing, and isolating. Not being ready, willing, or able to give up the addictive bulimic behaviors, I closed myself off to any form of recovery. The process was slow and first and I could still function and be successful, hiding bulimia and only allowing it at limited times. But as with any active addiction, left untreated, it will progress into fatal destruction. Leaving NA instead of honestly confronting my behavior, this untreated active addiction ultimately led me into an eventual return to drug use.

May 1998
Junior prom with Jesse Staples
6 months pregnant
Jesse broke up with me which started the
depression that led me to using drugs

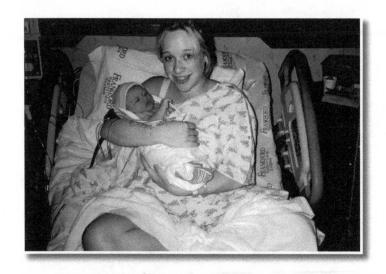

August 24, 1998
Laila is born

October 1998
My sister Beth, my brothers Matt and Joe

Halloween 1998

Thanksgiving 1998
I was back on drugs

June 1998
High school graduation
My mom, Laila and I
I left the graduation ceremony and went directly into rehab

May 2000
Laila and I
This was the day I came home from being away
for 5 months in long term treatment

August 24, 2000
Wildwood, NJ
I was 4 days clean…

Laila and those Teletubbies saved my life one afternoon

May 2004
Community College graduation
Almost 4 years clean

Laila and my Grandmom
My grandmom - an instrumental role model throughout my life

Winter 2005
Laila and I
Ski trip

Summer
Parasailing adventure

PART II

Regression

Slow Detachment

Many combined factors played a role in my eventual separation from Narcotics Anonymous and all were important pieces that I overlooked but should not have taken lightly. The moment I make myself different from others in recovery, you can no longer help me. I lose the connection of identification and the healing that results from this common bond.

Moving was the first of these changes that I could have been more prepared to face. I had no one explain to me the obstacles and challenges I was going to encounter so when I experienced problems or stress, I hid it. I figured I wasn't supposed to not know or be afraid and I didn't tell anyone. I had never before moved, had never helped anyone move, and yet I expected myself to handle it with a perfect calm. I was leaving my entire foundational support and venturing out—with a young daughter, into an entirely new and different area. On my own for the first time ever as a mother.

Although I plugged in with recovery during the first move, I didn't make the same effort to get and stay involved in Abington. Circumstances took over and I made excuses. Moving is similar to being a newcomer all over again—it takes a lot of work to connect in a new area. Reaching out for help, letting a new group of people get to know me, volunteering for service commitments, and cultivating new relationships. All while going to school, raising my child as a single mother, paying bills and living expenses, and working full-time. Looking at all the factors involved, moving requires a substantial group of solid and supportive friends. It cannot be done successfully alone. Such a huge transition calls for necessary effort on many people's part. I asked for no such support and berated myself when I found that I needed it.

Another important contributing factor was my newfound passion and involvement with school. It became my priority ahead of everything else. Although highly beneficial to my personal growth and development in many ways, I was out of balance. All my attention was on education. The constant interaction with academia led me to neglect another facet of my personality: addiction. And this area of my life needed attending to as much, if not more, than my desire to learn. I began to believe that I could "think" myself out of my problems. Wasn't I smart enough now? Look at all the knowledge I have now. I didn't realize that I had to divide my attention equally. My focus went to whatever I was interested in at the moment. At the cost of neglecting all other responsibilities.

About the time I was detaching from NA, I was also trying out different fellowships. I didn't know where I fit in or belonged or what group I wanted to be a part of. I would attend OA for help with the eating disorder and Al-Anon for apparent childhood anger issues. I even went to a few ACOA meetings. I was looking everywhere for a solution. Everywhere except exactly where I was. I felt scared, shaky, alone, and unsteady on my own. I didn't know how to do it. I had never lived in an adult world and I had no clue what was going on. That not knowing terrified me. Yet this I shared with no one. I was supposed to be a shining example in NA, I couldn't go to them with my problems.

Ultimately, moving away numerous times from a firm foundation of support plus placing my education at the top of my priority list combined with defocusing my commitment to NA by involvement with many other fellowships; all these factors contributed to my departure from recovery. All of these "life changes" could have been handled appropriately had I been willing to share honestly and allow others to help me. Instead, I took the reins in my own hands and pretended like everything was wonderful and great and perfect. No one warned me I was heading toward relapse because no one knew me. There wasn't anyone close to see the signs of downfall as I silently slid away from recovery. The deadliest denial of all is when I don't even know I am lying to myself.

I valued independence and self-sufficiency over the comfort and companionship of group support. Now that I was slowly detaching from NA, it became easier for addictive tendencies to creep back into my life. In my case, addiction does not merely creep. Rather, like a powerful force, it enters into my world and ransacks my life: quickly, silently, and destructively. Like a thief in the night, it steals my soul.

Slipping Away

Addiction hit with full force the weekend in October 2008 while I was away on the OA retreat. After the breakfast, when I walked into the bathroom and purged, I could have let it scare me enough to take corrective action. This could have been viewed as a red-light indicator that my program was in dire need of attention. It could have been a one-time, isolated incident that provided the catalyst to rocket me back into recovery. Or maybe I am not respecting the power of the disease. When does loss of control begin? Where and when could have I honestly made a different choice if I no longer had the power to choose. In retrospect, I say that I could have or should have or would have done things differently perhaps. But that is ego telling me that I could have beat the disease earlier. In reality, it already had me. That single slip opened up the floodgates of addiction that had been unlocked for some time. I resumed old behaviors with a vengeance.

Although I question whether or not I could have done anything differently, I did see disaster coming. In fact, any clear-minded observant witness to my life over the previous few weeks could and would have easily seen crisis approaching. I had all the signs of impending doom. I do not recall anyone ever pointing it out to me because even if they would have, by this point I was not receptive to anyone's advice. I often put on an "everything is great" mask—it was practically my self-image, so deeply engrained that I could not easily recognize the truth from the false. When I was not okay and pretending and when I was really all right inside were indistinguishable to me most of the time. I barely knew when I was pretending or being genuine. I could share easily and naturally in a way that impressed people, smile in a way that hid the secrets, and lie convincingly while staring into your eyes. So in all actuality, there was no one who could have forewarned me because nobody knew the real me. The hidden me was desperate, lost, and hopeless.

Who I was for the world was enormously different than who I was for myself and Laila. With others, I was exuberant, happy, cheerful, and radiant. My daughter knew the relentless side of me—harsh, critical, and demanding. Toward myself, I was horrendous—fake, guilty, and depressed. This incongruence, this façade I put on for the world, caused huge internal stress. If they only knew the real me…my worst fear: exposure. I lived anxiously and secretly, always avoiding close intimate relationships out of fear that you would discover what I already knew: I was a fraud. A complete fake—totally incompetent, unable to take care of myself, my life, Laila, or anything in the world. I didn't have it all together and I knew absolutely nothing about how to live and manage life. Especially deficient was I in the area of interpersonal connection. I knew not what to do with you or how to talk to you. Most importantly, I didn't know how to care about you. I was completely falling apart, swiftly and destructively. But I couldn't dare and wouldn't consider letting you know that. Ever.

No matter the cost, you were not to find out the real me that I kept so far hidden. What I was hiding from you, I was afraid to look at within myself. It takes extensive distraction to avoid yourself from yourself. Yet no amount of busyness, exercising, or studying could ever alleviate the nagging pain within. Then I remembered bulimia and this became my solution. Through total numbness, bulimia contained my secrets. A frantic stuffing of my inner shame followed by a violent release of the truth, forcing its way into existence. This cycle grew to monstrous proportions and although I repeatedly attempted help, bulimia had such a forceful hold that I was unable to let go even when I wanted to. Active addiction will take on a life of its own and eventually, take over my life. I was unable to change.

All addictions are characteristically the same in the following ways: (a) they get progressively worse—meaning the behavior becomes more drastic and severe; (b) tolerance builds up to the point where what used to be satisfying is no longer enough and continues on until the final stage where nothing of anything is enough; (c) preoccupation increases as the addiction demands more time and attention eventually becoming all-consuming; and (d) other areas of life are negatively affected until every area falls to total destruction. This is the most fertile ground for addiction—where there is nothing left but the addiction. No job, family, friendship, value, belief, money, or possession can withstand the absolute devastation of an untreated addiction.

Bulimia led me back to behaviors and beliefs that I had long ago put away. Lying and stealing, cheating and hiding, pretending and isolating. I was aware that I was downwardly regressing into becoming the person I used to be prior to recovery. Long before I was able to get honest or ask for help, it was clear to me that I was out of control. If not fully cognizant of the dangerous path I was on, I could see the breakdown of my thought process which culminated in a total defenselessness against sinking to another level of disease—picking up a drink again.

Mental Deterioration

*V*igilance is the key component in any long-term and successful recovery. Without proper support and attention, it is possible and probable to backslide into old and maladaptive behaviors, sometimes without even recognizing the regression. It is important to discover and identify "healthy" so that there is a mode for comparison and I can clearly distinguish "unhealthy" when it occurs. Mistakes are allowable and particularly in times of unexpected difficulties, it is easy to default back to old coping mechanisms. But when there is persistent action contrary to recovery, I rapidly return to the mindset I existed within prior to recovery. Gone are the skills practiced and cultivated over the years. Behavior follows thinking and thinking will follow behavior.

As I drifted away from Narcotics Anonymous, destructive ideas and thought patterns began to re-emerge. Without the skill of constant self-reflection called for in the steps or any accountability found in sponsorship, I was left to my own devices. My thinking got worse and darker as it led me deeper into the terrors of my untrained mind.

As Narcotics Anonymous became less important, materialism began to take precedence. My focus turned to success—achievement at all costs. My thoughts became centered on the pursuit of accomplishment—getting ahead, moving forward, attaining more, striving for excellence. Ambition took me to high places quickly, but at an even higher price.

Laila and I went from a roommate situation to an apartment to a house. A Saturn to a Nissan to a Volkswagen. An associate's to a bachelor's to a master's degree. These are normal and healthy progressive advancements. Expansion is a basic law of the universe. As we become responsible with a little, we are entrusted with more. The impact and influence we have on the world and those around us increases and expands. These stages are the customary markers for a naturally successful life. But they must be generated from within and reflect outward. In my life, the opposite was the case. I was making my internal self-worth dependent on external successes. I became driven to obtain and gain financially and materially at the expense of morality and virtue. It was suddenly acceptable to lie in order to get ahead, steal to obtain more, cheat for the quicker result. I wanted the "feel good" of accomplishment because that's all I had to cling to. Inside, I was desperate, frantic, searching. Outside, we had arrived.

Laila and I travelled the world together. We had every mate-rial luxury we had ever wanted. I had a beautiful home, which I lavishly decorated myself. I worked a stable job in financial services and had earned an MBA degree. To all outer appearances, we had it all. Occasionally, a family relative would ask if I was dating anyone. That was the only piece of our lives that anyone could "see" was missing. Although I had been single for almost my entire twenties, this rarely bothered me. I had a goal list to accomplish and a boy-friend had not even made it as an entry. I wanted to develop myself as a woman in recovery, establish myself as a single mother, grow in financial independence and freedom, build my career and receive an education. I wanted to be able to offer in a relationship exactly what I wanted from it—and I had high standards. So I put romance aside and stayed focused. As I progressively accomplished each goal I had set for myself, I would check it off the list and move right along.

No longer did my self-worth stem from a natural outpouring of self-reflecting step work. No longer did I value wholesome rela-tionships. My accomplishments made me who I was and all that mattered was success. Having thrown NA principles out the window,

I was running on my own juice. It would only be time before I ran out of steam. The useful life recovery had propelled me into would soon lose its momentum because I was not continuously supplying my engine (mind, body, spirit) with a healthy, adequate, or sufficient dose of fuel (recovery interaction). A car can only run for so long on fumes. In my case, my past growth, efforts, and change were driving my present day success in life but I did not realize that I was going to run out of gas. If I don't continue to make deposits into an account, eventually there's nothing left to withdraw. That is what happened in my recovery. For a bit, life remained steadily productive, then came to a brief standstill which was promptly followed by a rapid decline.

An active recovery keeps me accountable, focused, and aware. It constantly turns the attention to myself and my behaviors. It allows me to stay on top of my mistakes, be aware of lapses in judgment, negative or erroneous thinking, and keeps me reaching out to others when I find myself in a jam. Three important and extremely beneficial aspects of recovery are (a) involvement, (b) responsibility, and (c) service.

A) Involvement keeps me aware and reminded of addiction—who I am, used to be, and could become.
B) Responsibility holds me accountable for change.
C) Service removes my selfishness and provides fulfillment.

Recovery is a team effort—everyone's success depends on everyone else's success. I need you to get better and stay healthy and participate in recovery for two reasons: (A) You give me hope. If you are ahead of me in some way, I can look to you for support, direction, and guidance. The road does not have to be dark and lonely when another person knows the way and goes along the path with you. (B) You give me purpose. I can teach others by my example. My trials and pain are made worthy when they can be of value to another. To be useful and effective, I need you to need me. In this way, old-timers and newcomers alike play a vital role and share a mutual responsibility in recovery. Without the members with experience, newcomers would not be able to learn how to live clean. Without new people in recovery, old-timers would grow stagnant and forget where they used to be in addiction. Where we were, where we are, and where we want to be are three indispensable stages of recovery. I left in the middle before meeting my third responsibility of showing others the process I took to recover. Teaching others where we can go and who we can become through the steps is an exhilarating and inspiring experience. I bought the ingredients for the cake, baked it, but refused to share it now that it was cooked.

I also had the sense that I had "graduated" from Narcotics Anonymous. I had learned all that I could and would from NA and no longer had any use for it. I went through the steps twice, had been clean for more than double the amount of time I even used, and convinced myself that drug addiction was just a "teenage phase." This denial occurred over time as I slipped away from the recovery environment. It was intensified by my active involvement in the neighborhood, business, and educational communities. Once this belief of separateness had rooted itself, I had all but signed my own death warrant. When I think you different from me, I do not believe you can understand or help me. The healing power of identification is lost.

I had always been a superficial student. I love to master a subject's core concepts, understand its content, and move on. Commitment to any one field was never my flair. I've researched hundreds of areas this way in which I've had personal interest. I quickly change topics once I grasp a level of comprehension but never stay put in a single field to cultivate the thoroughness of expertise. Capable of absorbing and processing huge amounts of information, I would quickly devour a subject. I didn't view recovery in that way and for a while, it wasn't. Recovery had become a way of life, not a topic to be studied. I had for many years adopted recovery as a lifestyle.

Through academic study, materialistic priorities, and inattention to recovery, I began to view NA as just another subject that I had mastered. Add it to the list of experiences along with astrology, theology, tarot, Eastern religions of Buddhism and Hinduism, meditation, Reiki, massage, dream interpretation, neurobiology, brain functioning, I-Ching, Tao, esoteric philosophies, and psychology—just to name a few. Especially pertaining to the spiritual realm, you name it and I have probably studied it. I don't want to discredit knowledge, for I believe it is precious and valuable. Scientific research and experiential learning is a brilliant method of advancing civilization. But I had selfish motives for my learning—it was never about helping others or being a contribution to the world. I studied to "fix" myself. I came from a foundational belief of inherent brokenness. I was always striving to correct this faulty premise. I had thought NA would be the solution and in fact, the steps do lead me directly to the source: God and service to others. Having gotten caught up in the world of intellectualism, I had the brilliant idea that there may be a "new, different, and better" solution. And off I set to discover it.

I buried and distracted myself in a personal pursuit of perfection, unrealistic and improbable expectations, causing eventual destruction of myself and the lives of those around me. Instead of allowing my studies to complement my recovery, I made them more valuable. Left to my own devices, I will self-destruct. This is not an erroneous core belief or a pessimistic outlook. This is not a faulty or ignorant idea. It is not the result of childhood abuse or neglect and not the conditioned response of addiction. This is the center of my humanness and the foundation of my humanity. By myself, I am no good, do no good, think no good. I am entirely a social being, thriving only in an environment where I am surrounded by like-minded individuals, actively supporting and encouraging a group effort, common goals, and mutual understanding.

This happens naturally in the animal kingdom. When a member of the herd ventures off on its own, it loses direction, lands in enemy territory, and is powerless to withstand the attack without help. If there is no animal nearby to hear its cry for help, if it even attempts requesting help, that animal will perish at the hands of the enemy in a solitary fight for survival. It never should have left the support, care, and protection of its herd.

This is a comical illustration of the power of the NA group. Together, we can accomplish what we could never do alone. I need the group. I need others. I need to stay involved and connected to my source of life—the reason I have a life.

Romance

Prior to my downfall with bulimia, I was walking along the board-walk in Wildwood with Laila one afternoon during the summer of 2008 when a repressed, hidden inner longing arose so powerfully it almost knocked me to my knees. Things were perfect. Life was really, truly great. We had arrived earlier that morning for one of our special beach days. At the time we were living in Abington, in a cute little apartment. I was working toward my MBA. My job was secure and promising. Laila and I were holding hands and skipping past Ed's Funcade when it hit me—the forgotten pang of loneliness. I wanted to share this—this moment, this joy, this life, me, Laila. I had worked diligently to plan and create a beautiful life and here it was in this moment. Except with it came the overwhelming desire to give it away, to offer this to someone else. I wanted to share this life I had built for us. I suddenly felt selfish for keeping it to myself. I had grown to become a confident, successful, beautiful, spiritual, healthy woman. I was raising an amazing young daughter and together we thoroughly enjoyed life. And now, I wanted to share that with someone else. I no longer wanted our life to myself. Such began an interest in finding a compatible mate. I decided to date—I wanted a boyfriend!

Being the organized planner I always have been, I created an "Ideal Man" list, including anything and everything—major to minor, realistic to absurd. Qualities, beliefs, skills, education, personality, family history, interests, possessions, experience. It all was relevant. I listed every trait I could ever want. This way I could know it when he appeared in my life and see it if he didn't fit. Certainly not requiring 100 percent of my list met, very far from it. I simply needed to create a vision for myself and declare what was possible for me in a romantic relationship. It's useful when I know what I'm striving toward and I didn't want to be misled by fanciful feelings of infatuation. I took it on as a project. I've always viewed relationships as a mutual partnership. I like to know the roles and responsibilities up front with clearly defined expectations. Then I know how to succeed and that's what I like to do. I knew and believed that I had a lot to offer to a man and with this confidence, I set off in the pursuit of romance.

Armed with my "Ideal Man" list which I revised and updated every six months according to my newfound knowledge and experience within the course of dating, I now had a barometer by which to measure the men I was meeting. It was amazing! Once I made my request known to the universe and opened myself to the possibility of dating, men suddenly showed up everywhere. For over six years, I had rarely been approached by men and aside from two random one-night stands, had remained entirely sexually abstinent. I had no interest in developing a romantic relationship nor was I seeking male attention. Then, almost instantaneously after making the decision to find a boyfriend and turning my attention to the opposite sex, I was astonished at the results. I met men at the gym—that I had been attending daily for years! At the grocery store, men talked to me in the produce aisle. At work, there were requests for my number. Men approached me in airplanes and while on vacation. I dated men from my college classes and seminars I was involved in with Landmark. I met men in the neighborhood and at local community events. Even shopping at the mall, a man introduced himself to me at Yankee Candle. I enrolled in a ninety-day online social dating network. Needless to say, I had just as many men turn up there as in my daily interactions. During those three months, I had countless dinners, museum trips, coffee breaks, lunch hours, and strolls through the parks. The bar scene was of no interest because I knew I certainly was not going to meet a suitable mate with a drink in hand.

It's important to note the remarkable difference in the way I had previously viewed dating to the way I was maturely responding to men. I had been out of the dating game for many years, all the while growing, maturing, learning, and flourishing independently. There was no sense of "needing" a man—I was confident in my ability to successfully navigate life as a single mother. The codependency had been healed, and I was not looking for a man as a source of identity or self-worth. I was not attracted to or interested in "fixing" broken men. I now wanted an equal. I was also clear about what I wanted and it was a simple decision to move in a different direction and walk away if it wasn't found. Sex wasn't in the picture as I saw this as a time of investigation and discovery. This period of dating was a fun, social, and truly enjoyable experience. There were a few men who made a lasting impression on me and built the foundation for my future relationship desires. In other words, they taught me not to settle or to give up on what I want because the man of my dreams does exist, my ideal romance is realistic, and finding my perfect match is possible.

Mark

As a participant in a five-month-long Landmark class, I met Mark. He would sit next to me during our weekly sessions. I found him handsome and attractive but aloof and judgmental. During the length of the class, which is based on self-expression, Mark grew leaps and bounds. We soon exchanged contact information and were in communication frequently. He had graduated top in his class from college with a double major. He worked in finance as a partner at an investing firm. He was highly intelligent and classy. By the end of the five months, Mark was a smooth and sophisticated black suit businessman and I was interested.

He had theater season passes and VIP seating at five-star restaurants. He lived in an upper class section in the city. We talked about philosophy and he had a genuine desire to learn all about Laila. He took an annual ski trip to Aspen with his college roommates and every Thanksgiving was spent with family on Lake Michigan. He had traveled the world a dozen times over, backpacked through New Zealand for five weeks, and explored Alaska. He was powerful in the finance industry and knew how to generate wealth and profit. Mark was ambitious and the first man I ever dated that I could honestly describe as "emotionally mature." My favorite characteristic about Mark was that he was a "yes" to everything. I could mention the Tran Siberian Orchestra and we'd have tickets for the upcoming concert. I'd talk about a childhood bowling memory and we'd be at the alley the following weekend. He was open to having difficult conversations and engaged during our discussions. He didn't own a television. Fitness was a huge priority in his life and he founded a nonprofit youth group where he took under-privileged kids on outdoor adventures on the weekends.

I was twenty-six and he was thirty-two. We dated for a few months and I really enjoyed him. He showed me that what I want in a man is possible and real and available. I was still in college and we were in different life stages. I was young and developing while he was experienced and established. He actually said something to me when we parted ways that has stuck with me forever. He told me that I was a woman who could have any man she wanted but that I'm not done yet. He said that I needed a few more years of development. That was probably the most honest, insightful, and beneficial feedback I had ever received from anyone in my entire life.

I wasn't done maturing yet. I still had refining to do. I wasn't at the level where I was ready for a black suit Audi man. That is where I was heading and what I saw for myself in the future, but Mark had the tact to tell me directly: I'm not there yet. Over the years, we stayed in contact and kept tabs on each other. He later married and moved to the suburbs to raise their children in the manner he had envisioned for his family.

Dan

Months of actively dating a variety of men started to take its toll on me. I was beginning to feel frustration and doubting my vision of an ideal boyfriend. Would someone really come along who had what I wanted? Were my standards and hopes too high? My expectations unrealistic? In my heart, I didn't believe that my list was improbable but time and again, I'd come home after a date feeling disappointed.

Laila and I had our first Caribbean cruise scheduled for late spring 2008. It was the first ever Nickelodeon family cruise sponsored by Royal Caribbean cruise line. It was Laila's first time on a ship of this magnitude and her first time out of the country. This was a brand-new experience for us on many levels and we were exhilarated and enthused about our vacation together. We travelled to five different countries in a ten-day period, and to this day, it remains the single best week of my life. We were full of life and excitement and because of that, we attracted other single parent/kid teams who were also high-spirited and energetic. We still keep in touch with four people we met on that vacation and reminiscing about that experience brings back blissful memories for both of us.

Laila and I loved everything about being on the ship: the animal towels left by the amazing staff, the eleven levels of hallways and sleeping rooms. The massive size of the ship amazed us. Walking from one end to another, we would get captivated by shuffle board or jogging or the pools or rock climbing wall. We were selected to participate in a game show but were late getting back from our excursion of swimming with the stingrays in Grand Cayman. Nickelodeon chose a SpongeBob theme and Laila was in the final months of her SpongeBob stage. We enjoyed elegant meals and room service for breakfast. We watched a new and different theater presentation every evening. Laila swam in one of the four pools while I relaxed in the hot tub.

We brought waterproof wristwatches especially for this trip and we synchronized them every morning. In many ways, we were on our own at times, Laila liked the arcade and I enjoyed the yoga studio. Our watches ensured that we would both know exactly when we were meeting. I was unwilling to be worried for even a second over not knowing where Laila was. This was our first experience with trust. Every time we parted ways and headed off in different directions, we would confirm the time and location for when we were reuniting. This worked beautifully for us. Laila was excited because she experienced a new freedom and independence from me, yet she was still uneasy enough with it to be back precisely when her mother told her to.

Laila and I did it all. We shopped for hoodies and laughed until after midnight. She met Nickelodeon child celebrities and learned how to surf on the wave machine. I exercised in the gym every morning staring out at the infinite ocean before me. It was a week of grand extravagance and we would both be there again in a heartbeat. We canoed by hand to Dung River Falls and hiked the waterfall with hundreds of strangers in Jamaica. A native gave me a coconut as a parting gift, which customs took from me in the airport. We jumped off an inflatable volcano into the ocean on Paradise Beach in Mexico and slid down sixty-foot water slides in Haiti.

Here is where we met Dan and Melissa, a single father and his twelve-year-old daughter. I was twenty-seven years old and Laila was ten. Dan was older, handsome, and in phenomenal shape. We jogged past each other many mornings on the cruise deck track. Finally, on about day four of the trip, he approached me after a run as I was taking pictures of the sunrise from the back of the ship. We immediately connected. Perhaps the exhilaration of the cruise played a part in the rapid development of our elated romance. Whatever the external factors were, a part of me had been rejuvenated after meeting Dan. Something inside of me was re-inspired.

Dan had many of the qualities I was looking for in a man. I was hopeful again that my dream was possible and I was not "setting my sights" too high. Dan met and exceeded many of my expectations and even revealed traits that I would later add to my ideal man list. I was not naïve, however. We lived on different sides of the country and there was no solid commitment or expectation of a continuing exclusive relationship. The important thing was what meeting Dan reactivated in me: what I want is real. I will not give up on my efforts to wait for the ideal relationship to come along. I will not sell out due to self-doubt. When my heart envisions what it desires, it's important I trust that vision. I must continue pursuing my personal and individual goal. Don't settle for average when you want exceptional.

What exactly was it that Dan attracted and inspired in me? At first, it was his obvious commitment to fitness and a healthy, active lifestyle. He was handsome—tall and strong and muscular, smooth black hair with the graying streaks of maturity. He had the most mesmerizing piercing blue eyes that sparkled when he smiled. There was a definite physical attraction between us.

After spending time with him, the checklist continued to be completed. He was a former Marine colonel and had travelled the world a dozen times over during his service. He was now a military attorney in New Orleans, having put himself through law school while he was enlisted. Dan was intelligent and educated, well-traveled and worldly, successful and accomplished. He was established, financially secure, and ambitious with lofty goals and plans for his future. Dan's energy and enthusiasm matched my own. At fifty-two, he was older, wiser, and more experienced in just about everything and I greatly admired his knowledge and open-mindedness. Dan had an ex-wife and children. On this trip, only his daughter Melissa travelled with him, and she and Laila immediately connected. Because she was a bit older than Laila, they brought out different aspects of each other. At twelve years old, Melissa was developing interest in makeup and appearances and Laila enjoyed being a part of that. At ten years old, Laila kept Melissa connected to the children's activities at an age where she would not have participated by herself. They still remain friends on Facebook and keep in touch casually.

After connecting with Dan and Melissa, the four of us were inseparable. Dan and I would meet for breakfast in the buffet room after our workouts while the girls slept. We would take dancing lessons together in the afternoon while the girls enjoyed the cruise activities at the pool. The four of us sang karaoke in the recording studio, participated in hula contests, and cleaned up for the evening theater show every night after a fun-filled day of excitement.

Laila and I have always been a "yes" to life. We love new experiences, travel, and adventure. We had finally found another father/daughter team who shared our passion for living. There was nothing Dan was a "no" to. He painted ceramics with three females, rented a jet ski with me in Haiti, stared into the blackness of the ocean at midnight while holding my hand, wore a crazy hat for a contest, and brought us all jewelry at the gift shop in Jamaica. The Nickelodeon family cruise was a trip of a lifetime and renewed my hope in what was possible for myself, my life, and my relationships.

Before parting ways on our separate flights out of Miami, Dan, Melissa, Laila, and I shared a great lunch in a five-star hotel and strolled along Miami's South Side beaches. We hugged and cried and kissed our goodbyes. We were heading off to different places and it saddened me that Dan and I were in such drastically opposite stages of life. I was returning home to Philadelphia, where I was pursuing graduate school and embarking on a new career. Dan was going back to New Orleans, where he was preparing for an upcoming retirement of luxury and ease. I will always be thankful for my time with Dan because I saw through first-hand experience that maturity, stability, sincerity, power, enthusiasm, and success were all realistic traits. I didn't have to give up on my dream. Dan confirmed its existence.

Carl

In October 2009, Laila and I moved into our first house. We spent nine months in the housing market actively looking to buy. We probably walked through forty houses. We found a condo, placed an offer, and it was accepted. Laila and I packed up our tiny apartment and began purchasing items for our new house. We were thrilled as we both knew this was a huge step for us. Eleven days before settlement, the whole thing fell through. The zoning was not set up correctly and the mortgage could not be approved as FHA. There was no sale.

In frustration and resignation, I decided to consider renting. The perfect, ideal house was almost immediately presented and we moved in promptly. Everything was falling into place. Laila started middle school in Bensalem township. I had received my MBA degree earlier in the year and was actively pursuing advancement in my company. This was the way I met Carl, a business manager in a separate division of the company. I really wasn't much interested or attracted to him and I'm not sure why I initially agreed to date him. But I did. I was saying "yes" to life and didn't want to shut out an opportunity based on judgmental ideas. Even still, I found him to be highly critical, materialistic, superficial, harsh, cheap, entitled, and arrogant. The night I intended to end the continuation of our dating, he asked me if I'd like to take a trip to Costa Rica with him. Costa Rica is absolutely one of my favorite countries and I couldn't resist the offer. The beaches and mountains and jungles. I most definitely wanted to go again! Putting aside my decision walk away from a relationship with Carl, I asked for more details about the trip.

It turned out that we had an open invitation to his friend's villa for the week, complete with food and all necessities. A five-minute walk from the beachfront and unlimited use of the catamaran. All that we needed were plane tickets. How could I say no? I didn't. I said yes, even if it meant having to continue to date a man who I was not interested in. To be more accurate, a man I didn't even like. There was also an impulsive component to my decision—I had known Carl for only six weeks and was now agreeing to leave the country with him, and given only ten days' notice to do so. Airfare purchased, arrangements for Laila made, and in a week and a half's time, off to Costa Rica we went.

If I didn't like the guy while casually dating him, I really came to despise him while living in the same space as him. I tried not to allow my feelings to diminish my enjoyment of the country. We shopped, hiked, went ziplining, packed lunches for beach days, swam in the gorgeous ocean, and took the boat to the shores of Columbia. Costa Rica brings out an air of aliveness in me—it connects me with an ancient part of my soul and I feel overjoyed in the country. Yet in all this beauty and exuberance, I could not deny to myself any longer that I did not want to be with Carl. So one night, while dining on the beachfront restaurant, I told him I did not want to continue our romantic involvement upon returning home to the US. I explained that I wanted to enjoy the rest of our trip as friends and part ways on good terms at home. I felt instant relief after being honest with myself and him.

His reaction was not what I had expected. Carl became moody and obnoxious to the point where I was about to get up and leave the restaurant. It was more than clear that a relationship would not ever work between us. As I was about to say goodbye and walk away from the table, a waiter came by with a pineapple full of a frozen drink. I mentioned how delicious it looked; I had always been a fan of smoothies and fruit is top favorite food group. Carl started reading off all the fruity alcoholic beverages available on the menu and questioned why I had yet to order a single drink all week.

I explained to him that I didn't drink, hated alcohol, and in fact, through the entire length of my life had only ever had one experience with putting alcohol in me. Carl began telling me about the types and varieties of drinks that I could start off with as a "beginner." I turned my head to gaze at my surroundings. There was a beautiful sunset on the horizon of the ocean. Sand was rubbing my toes through my sandals. The orange sky was majestic. Palm trees sprouted every ten feet. Looking around at the beauty and elegance of this exotic country, I thought, "This will be okay. I have never drank before and these drinks look yummy. I'll try one." I ordered a pina colada.

I remember sipping it and thinking, "Wow, I just lost my clean time. Nine years plus over." It had been so long since I had been committed or involved in NA that clean time no longer mattered to me. Recovery was no longer an important source of esteem and accomplishment. I drank the pina colada and ordered a second frozen Mohito drink. I loved them both. Instantly, I felt the warmth from the alcohol slide into my belly. I suddenly felt giddy, flirty, silly, talkative, and completely at ease with a man I couldn't even stand. I enjoyed our conversations, remembering not at all what we spoke of. I laughed and conversed as if on a date with the man of my dreams. Yet it was entirely alcohol induced. Those drinks gave me the ability to be who I couldn't be without them: in denial, lying to myself, and pretending I liked Carl.

When we went back to the house that night, I slept with Carl for the first time. A man I didn't like, couldn't wait to be away from, and wanted no future involvement with. A man I had just told three hours earlier that I was ending our romance. In a single evening with alcohol, I compromised everything I had built myself upon for the last eight years of sexual abstinence. Purity had become precious to me and I gave myself to Carl without even thinking. Alcohol decides my standards for morality, dignity, and respect. At the time, I was more upset with myself for sleeping with a man I couldn't stand than for relapsing because in fact, I loved the effect those drinks had on me. The ease and warmth and comfort the alcohol produced in me had me ready for more. The disease had been reactivated.

PART III

Relapse

10

Picking Up

*T*he remainder of the vacation spent in Costa Rica with Dan was awkward and uncomfortable. Departing from the plane, it was with anticipated relief that we both went our separate ways. The trip was over, but a new chapter of my life was just beginning. In a single evening, I gave up my clean time and sexual abstinence. I didn't yet have a strong, overpowering urge to drink again, but I also knew that I would not decline alcohol in the future.

It was about a month later that I attended my tenth year high school reunion. I made it clear to a few people that it was only my second time ever drinking. They quickly informed the bartender to take it easy on the liquor in my drinks. I asked an old high school friend to select fruity drinks for me, and he stayed on top of his assignment. All night long, I had one drink in my hand after another. I barely remember the event. Within less than an hour, I was totally drunk, falling down in the bathroom and constantly forgetting where I put my purse. At the end of the night, I stumbled to my car, literally falling in the parking lot on the way. I remember feeling embarrassment as I overheard two classmates laughing at me. They watched me hobble to my car, get in, and drive away in that condition. The car ride home I had to close one eye while driving because the double vision made it impossible for me to see straight. I was scared, really scared. At that moment, I knew I was out of control drunk and the only thing I could do was wait for it to pass. Thus ended drinking experience number two.

A few weeks later, at a birthday dinner for my dad, I ordered a vodka and cranberry at the restaurant. The alarm and shock on the faces of my brother and father was unsettling. The hounding questions began: "Am I sure I want to do this?", "Do I think this is a good idea, given my history?", and finally, "Why, after all this time?" I only ordered two drinks that night but a drastic change had occurred: I had a definite craving for more.

It was New Year's Eve when I intentionally decided to enter a liquor store and purchase alcohol for myself. I had a Kahlua drink earlier that evening at a friend's party but I did not stay to ring in the New Year. I was driving home to an empty house by myself before midnight. Laila was spending New Year's Eve at a sleepover and I was alone. I had never stepped foot into a Wine and Spirits shop before in my life. I didn't know what to expect or what to select. I asked the cashier where the vodka was and I selected the largest bottle of Three Olives Mango flavored vodka. Having drank vodka less than a handful of times, I had never made a drink and didn't know anything about appropriate amounts. Not that I cared, I was drinking to get drunk and be drunk as quickly as possible. I decided on fifty-fifty—half vodka with half cranberry juice. I drank out of normal twelve-ounce drinking glasses, which meant that I was drinking ¾c of vodka and ¾c of cranberry juice. That did the trick. This is how I drank: holding my nose and gulping the liquid down my throat. I don't know how much I drank that night because I don't remember anything after taking a shower, which I did directly after pouring my second fifty-fifty drink. I was a blackout vodka drinker from the first time I poured myself a drink. And I liked it that way.

I don't drink like a lady, not politely or gracefully and never socially or leisurely. I force mouthfuls of disgusting-tasting, foul-smelling vodka down my throat in an attempt to get it over with as quickly as possible. It's the feeling I am seeking, not the experience of drinking. I want only the drunk. I drink as fast as I can, as much as I can handle until I can no longer stand. Why do I drink? Because I want to experience the effect that alcohol produces for me.

After New Year's Eve, I kept vodka in stock at my house. Immediately after coming home from work, I'd have a drink—always one of my fifty-fifty homemade drinks. Soon, my family started to express concern. So as to not worry anyone, I began to hide the bottles and sneak the drinks. I kept at least six twenty-ounce Powerade bottles in my refrigerator at all times with "Mom" written on them in permanent marker. I told Laila they were mixed with Red Bull so that she wouldn't try to drink any. And there was Red Bull in the drinks—Red Bull, vodka, and juice, but mostly vodka. I was soon taking these bottles with me everywhere—to work, shopping trips, in the car, and family visits. No one suspected that I was drinking because it looked like Powerade juice. I always had one or two bottles with me. I learned to plan ahead because I was afraid I'd run out and be forced to sober up.

There is an entire six-month period of my life that I do not remember. Laila would get annoyed with me because I often knew nothing about what was said or done the previous day. This was a daily, continuous pattern. Once I started drinking, within six weeks' time, I became a daily blackout vodka drinker, having to be drunk at all times and for everything. And I kept it all a secret. From the very first night I poured myself a drink in my own home, my drinking behaviors were sneaky and hidden. I stayed isolated and alone. When there was a family picnic, neighborhood party, or a work event, I would actually have my own bottle of vodka in my purse so that nobody would notice how much I was drinking. Drinking was rarely a social activity for me—I was not drinking to cultivate friendships. I wanted to be drunk.

In February 2010, I ran into an old high school classmate. I had seen him at the reunion a few months prior but we hadn't engaged in much discussion. This time, we met at a bar where we had both come to listen to a local band. He told me that he wasn't going to let me leave again without asking for my number. We flirted and danced and talked all evening. He called a few days later, and we scheduled our first dinner date. This was the outer Sara that Brian met and saw and fell in love with: beautiful, alive, energetic, charismatic, and successful. This was the hidden Sara that I didn't allow him to see until it was too late: hopelessly bulimic, actively alcoholic, and suicidal, lost, and falling apart.

During our first evening out, I sensed something special about Brian. I felt immediately at ease in his presence. He was gentle and loving, generous and funny. He brought out a part of me that was comfortable and sensuous. We shared all of the same beliefs and values and wanted similar things in life. Our personalities were highly compatible. I liked to be the center of attention and he was the backstage kind of guy. I was outgoing and energetic while Brian was good-natured and easy-going. His stability grounded me and my enthusiasm kept him inspired. We were a great team together. He was looking for a long-term commitment and I was ready for a boyfriend. I intuitively knew from that first night that the relationship was going to work.

President's Day weekend, Laila and I had a ski trip planned at the Poconos. I invited Brian to come along. I wanted him to meet Laila and I wanted to see how Laila responded to him. We planned for a day trip, leaving early and coming home late. The car ride up to the mountains was fun—Lalia had a friend with her and everyone was in high spirits. The skiing itself was hilarious and a total blast. Laila and I had been going skiing about twice a year since she was five years old so we were reasonably strong skiers. On the other hand, both Brian and Laila's friend Julie were not as experienced. Not that Laila and I are anywhere near professional but we do usually ski at least one black diamond run. It was funny skiing with beginners. We laughed and fell and teased each other. We bonded and created enjoyable memories. This was a brand-new kind of excitement for Laila and myself also. She rarely, if ever, met anyone I was dating and never before had Laila participated in a date with me. It was time though, as everyone was ready and hoping to join as a family. My internal senses had been accurate that first evening. There was something special about Brian.

One factor involved in the quickly developing relationship with Brian was the pre-existing common ground we shared having gone through high school together. Although we had never been friendly or social during those years, we did share quite a few classes and knew of each other. Other common denominators that brought us closer were our similar mind-sets about important relationship issues. We both valued family tremendously. He had a young child from a previous girlfriend and his commitment to fatherhood was genuine and impressive. We both wanted our future to consist of children, dual income, vacations, and college funds. We both had great potential for advancement in our careers and were actively pursuing promotions. And there was an irresistible sexual attraction between us. Brian was simple to please, easy to get along with, and agreeable to suggestions. I could talk to him about work, feelings, dreams, or science. He enjoyed being active in the outdoors. The sincerest part of Brian was that he honestly admired and respected me and paid special, unconditional attention to Laila.

It had started snowing on our way home from the ski trip. We arrived at my house very late in the evening and we decided it would be okay if Brian spent the night on our couch instead of driving home in the snow. We made a joke later because as it would turn out, Brian would not leave after that first sleepover. He belonged with us. It snowed all through the night and became a severe blizzard, keeping me, Brian, Laila, and her friend Julie trapped in the house together for three days. The conditions were so awful that a state of emergency was declared, schools and businesses were closed, and the four of us were forced to share hot chocolate, snowball fights, and movies together. Brian never spent another night at his apartment after that ski trip. It sounds amazing and shocking even thinking back on it, as it was so early in our relationship but that was day Brian moved in. And you know what? Laila and I wanted him to.

As the weeks progressed, we loved having Brian around. There was a special energy in our home as the spirit of love engulfed us. We found that three people at the dinner table gave us more stories to share. Sitcoms became entertaining because they were a family activity. After the long search, the many years, innumerable dates, and dragging loneliness, Brian was here. Falling in love was extraordinary for me and Laila experienced the benefits also. She was delighted to have Brian in the house. They shared a mutual understanding and a formed a natural and easy bond. Sensing Brian's sincerity and goodness, Laila easily came to trust and care for him. And Brian adored Laila. They would share secrets and make fun of me. It thrilled Laila to have such a loving man in her life, paying attention and loving her. Their relationship was rewarding and fulfilling for me to watch. It warmed my heart to see my Laila opening up so naturally and willingly. When I became pregnant at sixteen, it was not a personal decision. I did not intentionally select the man with whom I wanted to have a child. Laila's biological father was not stable or mature enough to be a dad, so I promised Laila that I was going to give her an exceptional example of a father. And Brian was that dad for her.

With Brian in our lives, our dreams had come true. We were living love, experiencing joy, and feeling happiness. It was the culmination of years of trial and errors, selectivity, elimination, and refinement. Brian completed our world and we offered him the same fulfillment. In the midst of all this abundance, however, there was an array of deceit clouding the entire relationship. I was in a deep state of denial, heavily drinking, and consumed by a debilitating eating disorder—all of which I kept secret. My primary disease has always been bulimia. I developed alcoholism as a result of an untreated eating disorder. I could stay clean in a recovery fellowship for years without ever working on my core issue. And I would appear to be doing well while falling apart inside.

I was lying to myself as I tried to ride on my laurels, run off the years of previous recovery, and convince myself that I could still be the same woman. In truth, I was no longer an honest, caring, joyful, successful, attractive, radiant woman. I was desperately pretending to be, clinging to every last vestige of composure, frantically showing the world a face of success and integrity. But I am not privileged to have the ability to maintain denial for any extended period of time. I knew the truth. Addiction had me the second I resumed bulimia. The associated behaviors came back with a vengeance and I returned to lying, stealing, sneaking around, isolating, and hiding. I made a heroic attempt to appear normal, well-adjusted, put together, and coping successfully with the challenges of life. I always knew better: I was on the road to destruction, already halfway to the gates of hell.

In this respect, I was also dishonest with Brian. The relationship took off so fast that I was able to fool him, for a while. He fell in love with the girl I used to be because that is who I showed to him. I was no longer that girl and with the progressive deterioration of addiction, it was only a matter of time before Brian realized this. At first, it was only bulimia that was a noticeable problem. It's difficult to live with someone in a bulimic addiction such as mine and not become aware of it.

The vodka addiction was still being carefully hidden in water bottles and mixed Powerade drinks. When the eating disorder did finally got his attention; I confessed and agreed to enter into an inpatient psychiatric unit for treatment. Brian stood by my side throughout the entire painful process. He was loyal and loving, faithful and compassionate. We had family therapy sessions together where we openly discussed supportive measures that could be taken to assist me in my recovery journey. However, the transition home was not peaches and cream. I binged on oatmeal that very night and threw it all up. And so the cycle began again. I was in a hopeless condition and unable or unwilling to break the bulimic lifestyle.

Then the drinking began to worsen. Brian started to complain of my near-nightly blackouts and there was more than one trip to the ER for alcohol poisoning. At this point, I was taking alcohol to work with me and frequently attending after work happy hours. Life was falling apart and I didn't know how to make it stop.

It was during our family vacation to California where my drinking took a turn for the worse. Cali was a 24-7 drink fest. We stayed with Brian's relatives and of the parts I can remember, the trip was fun and enjoyable. Disney Land, Sea World, beach days, shopping. However, it was here in California when I decided I was going to use cocaine again. Drinking wasn't enough for me anymore. I searched on foot as far as I could in the local town for some coke, but Brian kept intersecting, making my attempts unsuccessful. So I decided to save all the money I had left and not spend any more cash on vacation. I would buy cocaine the moment I stepped off the plane in Pennsylvania. I knew where to get drugs in Philly. This will work. Plus, another bonus: Laila and Brian were on a different flight home than me and they would be returning to the house about six hours after I had already arrived. So I had some leeway. This was good. This was my plan.

I stepped out of the airport. Without Brian or Laila around, I felt a nervous anticipation in the pit of my belly. I was on my way to get high. I remember the excitement and fear of that old, familiar drive down 95, getting off at the Allegheny exit. I had not been on this road in over ten years, yet I remembered the name of the street I used to buy cocaine on: Randolph. I bought $300 worth of cocaine that afternoon, began to snort it in my car on the way home, and immediately recalled the exhilaration I had once, so long ago, found in those lines of powder. Here again, I had found the answer. This was it. I was now using after a decade clean and I was committed to doing everything in my power to stay on a cocaine high forever. This deadly reunion with my first love made everything all right again. The world made sense and I was okay. However, my intuition knew: this was bad. Very, very bad, and it was going to go downhill at a rapid rate. I don't use drugs moderately or socially—I am not even interested in those concepts. Cocaine had me in its grips again and I willing surrendered my soul. Yet in the back of mind, I always knew I was headed for trouble. Disaster awaits.

Progression

July 2010

*T*wo weeks into using, I knew it was time to go back to NA. I needed help again. I was using as often as I could, which was almost daily. I was leaving work on lunch breaks and driving to the city to cop. Coming back to work, I would snort lines on my desk in the office. Brian knew I had used cocaine at least once in the last two weeks, but he was extremely unaware of the extent of my use. I was hiding it, using as soon as I woke up and then at night, drinking vodka to come down and fall asleep. I was scared, really scared because I knew where drugs took me, but the attraction to the pleasure of cocaine was so powerful that I didn't feel willing to give it up. It was enough for me to return to NA, so back to meetings I went. But meetings without desire won't get me clean and I continued to use. I took a leave of absence from work, put myself in an eating disorder clinic, and obtained thirty full days clean! However, I did not end the bulimic behaviors and eventually returned to cocaine very shortly.

August–September 2010

During these months, I continued to use, now spending all of my money on drugs. Savings, paychecks, all available funds were going to my next fix. I was still paying bills, but Brian and I were fighting constantly: I was taking all the money, I was still actively bulimic, and I was barely trying to get clean again anytime in the near future. I was making feeble attempts to participate in NA. Life was getting worse, not better, as addiction promises. Brian was on the brink of moving out because of my actively using. I was out of control and unwilling to change. I knew I was in big trouble. By the end of September, Brian had had enough. He worked in county corrections and living with an active addict jeopardized his career. And he had other children that he had to be a role model for, and I was far from being a healthy mother figure. So he left.

October 2010

At this point, just a few months into a cocaine relapse, I checked into rehab. I stayed eleven days but the bulimia became so uncontrollable that I had to be medically discharged from the facility. Upon my release, I headed directly to North Philly and was high within three hours of leaving rehab. This also happened to be the last month I paid any bills. A credit score of 785 was quickly about to be flushed down the toilet. Still out of work on disability, having spent all my savings, I needed every last dollar for drugs. Cable, water, rent, and electric no longer mattered.

November 2010

This was a bad month. I was clearly unemployable, unable to do anything but get and use drugs. I resigned from my job and was approved for unemployment. More free money. That same week, I crashed and totaled my beloved car. With no savings or substantial income, I could not afford repairs or a new vehicle. I saw the destructive progression: I was now losing valuable and important things. Material things that meant something to me. Brian had moved out, I had no job, and now my car was gone. I was paying no creditors. My rent, cell phone, and cable bills were the only ones I really cared about and even they went by the wayside at this point. I was noticeably falling apart: my family was concerned, bulimia was debilitating, and I had now started using heroin instead of vodka to come down from the cocaine. I was up for days, barely paying attention to Laila, consumed only with using more of my substance.

December 2010

I was going through money insanely; I couldn't afford my daily cocaine and heroin habits. In late December, I woke up to find twelve to fifteen relatives in my living room. My mom had hired an interventionist, and this was my family's ultimatum: get help or we are done with you. Surrounded by aunts, uncles, cousins, and siblings, I agreed to return to rehab. Off I went, two days before Christmas, back to another treatment facility. Bulimia was active but I hid it and did not mention it to the counselors, due to my fear of being discharged again. With a full-blown drug addiction, bulimia had taken somewhat of a backburner importance. I was gaining weight due to not purging constantly, but continuing to eat like an active bulimic. I gained ten pounds in my sixteen-day stay at Mirmont. I left armed with my debit card, which contained a previous unemployment deposit. My brother picked me up from treatment, I convinced my mother to let me use her car "to go to a meeting"...and off to Philly I went. Again, I was high within three hours of my departure.

January–March 2011

I had enough. This had to stop. I was hurting Laila, losing everything, deeply backsliding. I decided I wanted my clean date to be January 11, 2011. So on January 10, I used for the last time and committed myself to recovery. I now fully believe that our sober dates are assigned by God. I got a sponsor, went to meetings daily, worked steps, shared...and got a boyfriend. Not throwing up as often as in the past, but still overeating, I was also quickly gaining weight. I stayed clean for sixty days and life began to improve, but I had gained another twenty pounds. And on my sixtieth day clean, I had my mom's car and extra money. I got high once again before going to an afternoon meeting with my boyfriend, where you could find me in the bathroom, snorting lines of cocaine and heroin.

April 2011

Life got worse. I began pawning my electronics, stealing from family, and taking Laila's allowance money. My associates became old friends from Croydon, people I had gotten high with as a teenager but hadn't seen for over ten years. I struggled in NA, becoming the girl "to stay away from." I couldn't get clean and I was in bad shape. I was hanging out with the wrong people. At one point, I even allowed my daughter's father to stay with us because I needed the $100/week he "promised" to give me. Life was bad, but I had no idea how bad they were about to get.

May 2011

Next, we lost our house. My prized possession. We didn't get evicted because I wasn't paying the rent (I actually was), but the landlord was in NA and had said I needed to move out if I couldn't/wouldn't stay clean. She showed up with a drug test one afternoon, which I failed because I had been getting high that whole day, and she told me it was time to go. My rent was paid until the fifteenth of the month, leaving me nine days to pack up an entire house, yard, porch, and basement. Thank God for cocaine. I didn't sleep, stayed high and speeding the entire time. Moving everything into a storage unit, I rented a U-Haul truck and asked some NA friends to help me load/ unload. My family would have nothing to do with me and although I could handle the packing, I know I could not lift the furniture or drive a twenty-foot truck. Heartbroken, ashamed, and devastated, I moved my daughter in with my mother and I was heading back to rehab, to be followed by a long-term halfway house. On Saturday, May 14, 2011, three friends showed up and loaded/unloaded a truckful of my belongings into storage. However, it was an entire house that needed to be moved and was going to take two more truckloads to complete. The friends left after the first trip. When they left, I had absolutely no one—no help and no way to do it on my own. I was completely alone. Hysterical, high, overwhelmed, and full of despair, I sat down and sobbed. I was done. This is what addiction had taken from me. I have nothing. I have no one. I am alone. I was beaten and I knew it. Even my NA friends wanted nothing to do with me at this point, indicated by the total lack of help and support I received with the move. An old neighbor finally did show up, and together, he and I unloaded the final truckload into the unit. We went to my mom's house to drop off Laila's furniture and belongings, since she was now going to be residing there. I had abandoned her for drugs and rehab.

There was no one to drive the massive U-Haul truck, since my old neighbor had driven his own car to my house. Through tears, I agreed to drive—clearly knowing that I was unable to handle this giant vehicle. Turning off a corner street and onto the main road, I went under a bridge. I misjudged the alignment and swiped the entire side of the truck along the bridge, causing major damage, igniting the air bag which filled the cab of the truck with smoke and fumes, and ultimately, totaling the U-Haul rental truck—on which I had declined the $17 insurance coverage. Now uncontrollably hysterical, with my friend right behind me in his truck, we pulled over and waited for the tow. The tow truck took the U-Haul, full of my now broken and damaged furniture, to my mother's house. Most items were shattered or destroyed by the impact of the crash. To make matters worse, numerous aunts and uncles had stopped by mom's house that afternoon for an unexpected visit. What a sight! Here I am, at my weakest, lowest state ever—utterly humiliated in defeat—and my relatives had to be there to see it. I was devastated, destroyed, done. And I was exhausted, not only from being up for nine days on cocaine or from packing up an entire house. My inner being was tired, worn out from the drug lifestyle. I wanted recovery. I needed rest. Off to rehab I went.

I slept for seven full days in Fairmount detox, awakening only for medication and meals. I couldn't shower, change my clothing, exercise, or brush my teeth. I had neuropathy in my fingers which lasted six weeks, from toxins in the cocaine. When I finally came out of hibernation, I was forced to attend groups with the rest of the community. Yet I was also severely depressed, a major component of stimulant withdrawal. I cared little about anything, barely participated, and was unable to sit long enough to focus or concentrate—not that I had any desire to do so. I simply wanted to not use drugs and clear up my head a bit. Plus, I was now homeless, so long-term treatment seemed like the most logical solution. However, I met a guy. I had never had a "rehab romance" before and frankly, didn't much care to, but this guy showed me attention. I was lonely, battling a debilitating depression, and eating constantly. (I gained an additional twenty pounds in that rehab—mostly in the detox stage where I only ate and slept for over a week.) I started hooking up with this guy in rehab and suddenly, the days seemed a little more enjoyable. He talked constantly about shooting coke. Me, I snorted coke and heroin. I hated needles, was disgusted by blood, and totally repulsed watching people inject around me. However, one afternoon, I had the brilliant idea that before I got clean—permanently, totally clean for good and forever—I wanted to see what shooting cocaine felt like. I would use for a few days and head back to the halfway house. This guy and I decided to leave rehab together to go shoot coke. After three weeks in Fairmount—my longest stay yet at a facility, we walked off the grounds together. I had unemployment paychecks saved up in my bank account so we stopped at the local ATM and took a cab to Philly. If I could take back anything in my whole life, it might not even be that initial pina colada in Costa Rica. It very likely would be my decision to leave rehab to shoot cocaine.

June 2011

This is the point-of-no-return month. Life now progressively gets worse on a *daily* basis, whereas up to here I can sort of categorize the destruction monthly. That no longer is effective. Jose and I rented a motel room for a week and I shot cocaine. Nothing will ever be the same. The second the needle went into my skin, I knew I would never snort anything ever again. And I was also aware that there was absolutely nothing I would not do for that feeling. All bets were off, all limits were gone. Nothing could stand in the way of continuing to shoot coke. I needed it. I loved it. I had to do it.

There are stages of addiction and injecting cocaine skyrocketed me into the final, late stage—where there is no consequence too great and no behavior too extreme. There becomes no length to which one will not go in order to get, use, and continue to stay high. Cocaine, speedballs, heroin. I was shooting up ten to fifteen to twenty times a day and my arms were starting to get track marks. I hadn't called my mom after leaving rehab, and I started to feel bad. So one afternoon, about three days into the motel stay, I rang her phone. She thought it was a ghost on the other line. I heard it in her voice—she thought I was dead. She called the rehab and they told her that I left with a guy. My mom had been calling morgues and hospitals for two days. This is what addiction does. This is the agony and suffering with which it tortures others. A mother thought her daughter was dead. She had already told my sister and the church.

Within a week, Jose had assaulted and robbed me and I was once again broke and homeless. I cried to my mother, terrified by the power of the injection. I was truly scared. I had no control and couldn't stop. I went back to detox, of course. My form of a temporary reprieve. After six days, I left again AMA (against medical advice) and took a cab to Philly. Getting high in North Philly, getting robbed by a dealer, hiding under bridges to shoot drugs, and walking the streets alone looking for more. These were daily components of my everyday life. It was awful. I was pathetic. With no money and no way home, my mom and sister once picked me up in Kensington, so I could at least be in my hometown. No longer allowed to enter my mother's house, a few of the nights she let me sleep in her car, on Laila's trampoline, or on her porch swing. It was June, so being homeless on the streets, sleeping outside at night was still okay for me. There weren't any standards of living left. I was watching as unacceptable circumstances became acceptable. I was now afraid of myself. I was absolutely untrustworthy—stealing and robbing from anyone I could anytime I got the chance. The pawn shop clerks knew me and I now also knew the public transportation routes—the train, the El, and the city buses. I saw Laila two or three times during the entire month and every time I was high—a distracted, inattentive, lousy, pathetic excuse of a mother.

I also discovered my own personal doom: I call it the "borderline experience." The first time it happened, I was terrified, then I didn't consider myself to be high enough without it. It happens when there's too much cocaine in the syringe and you "fish out." There's a deep, intense "whooshing" vibration throughout the whole body, beginning immediately by pushing the syringe into the vein. Everything spins, turns black, and echoes loudly. Only repeating aloud the name of "God" could bring me out of it. I loved it. It was crossing over to the other side, jumping off the cliff and coming back. It's a borderline seizure experience and it occurred eight times during the course of twelve days. I could now no longer get high without seizing up. It was my everything. Even as I write this, my hand is shaking uncontrollably, my heart is in a state of terror and panic, and my belly is screaming with anxiety of recalling the experience. It's the single most powerful force in existence for me. I was intentionally putting lethal amounts of cocaine into the needle because this was how I had to get high now. Anything less was worthless. I wanted to die—desperately trying to end my life this way—but every time... something, *not me*, would force me to call out "God" over and over again until I would come back. I rarely wanted to come back, but I was compelled to cry out to God and return. This happened continuously. Daily, sometimes hourly. This is how I use: tragic, deadly, hard. And this was only a month into shooting coke.

July 2011

This month I made two friends. First, I ran into a guy from NA who had recently relapsed after thirteen months clean. He had tried to help me get clean around Christmastime of last year. We ran into each other while buying drugs on the same corner in Philly. Me, cocaine; him, crack. He still had his car, job, and apartment and invited me to stay with him. I readily accepted, being broke and homeless. We used constantly and we used hard. I also met a guy at a gas station, who had his own place and his own business. He lived a few streets away from my mother's house. He was letting me stay with him also. I told him about my cocaine problem one afternoon and he was trying to help me, to "save me." I was stealing from him and using him, taking full advantage of his kindness and naivety. He didn't know what he was getting into, as a ravaging addict, I soon terrorized his life. He'd tell me I had to go, then I'd come back begging for a place to stay. I'd lie about going to rehab or going back to NA or getting a job (that one was laughable), and he'd always give in.

My NA friend and I also became involved in crime during this month. This was absolutely the beginning of the end. I needed to fund my blazing cocaine addiction and was ready to accept any means necessary in order to do so. The world of crime opened up to me, and I readily entered. I was arrested for the first time on July 22, 2011, and because I had no address to go home to, the district judge sent me to jail. I spent six days in jail after which my bail was lowered to $100, and I deeply conned and manipulated my father to get me out. Similar to being released from every other facility, I was high again within three hours of hitting the street. The whole time in jail, I slept, awakening only to eat. I could not wait to shoot coke again and kept fantasizing vividly about the borderline experience. The rituals of using also occupied my thoughts: the coke bags, the water bottle lids, the cotton, the needles, the blood drawback, finding the vein, and then…injection. My heaven. I was consumed with shooting drugs and even six days in jail did not deter me. There were few—if any—consequences of addiction that were no longer acceptable to me. Substandard levels of living and unpredictable, violent circumstances were okay with me. I was also now a frequent visitor to our local ERs. With abscesses on both arms, I was humiliated. I sobbed, cried, and agreed to go to rehab again. My NA friend agreed to get clean with me too. He had taken me to the hospital and visited me during my five-day stay. I had surgery on both arms and was placed on IV antibiotics. I was tested for every disease and infection. It was a staph infection, non-MRSA and needed to be properly cared for upon my release. On my third day in the hospital, I decided that I wanted to use again. The obsession hit me and I answered. But now my arms were inaccessible for injection use. A friend from my past, that ex-boyfriend Joey, was home and back in town on a weekend furlow from work release. He taught me how to inject into my neck. This didn't always work for me, so I was also injecting straight into the abscesses. I wound up in the hospital three more times this month. Twice I had operating room surgeries. I had a total of five abscesses and had cellulitis twice. I was not skilled at injecting drugs and at this point in my using, I no longer had anyone around me who could do it for me because I was too much for most people. I was constantly shooting drugs, all day long, every day. I was addicted to the needle. Hopelessly. Desperately. When I didn't have drugs to shoot, I would inject water just to stick a needle in me. But I was terrible at doing this, so it left me with scars, bruises, and infections constantly. Twice, while in the hospital, after just having had OR surgery, still on IV antibiotics, with bleeding wounds and open abscesses—I ripped the IV line out of my hands in the middle of the night, leaving AMA. I would get a ride from my using buddy, the NA friend—now my crime partner, and we would flee the night bringing destruction all around us. My mother, barely holding it together and having given up on me, worried constantly that sepsis infections would get into my bloodstream, attack my heart, and kill me instantly. I couldn't have been so lucky. I wanted to die. I had given up on intentionally trying to overdose because that apparently wasn't working, I was overdosing daily and still alive. I couldn't live and also refused to get clean. It was despair and hopelessness compounded a million times—sheer, utter, brutal apathy. I just didn't care.

Now I'm involved in crime daily, becoming acquainted with the happenings of night crawlers, I see clearly why normal, healthy people sleep during the hours of 1:00 a.m. to 4:00 a.m. Atrocities occur. Horrendous, unimaginable ideas seem brilliant. The insane becomes practical. I now lived in this subculture, the realm of the undead—those of us no longer living but still somehow breathing. No one should know this existence. There is no sense of humanity or normalcy; rather, this is the land of depravity, desperation, degradation, humiliation, and death. This is where I found myself at the end: morality gone, law meaningless, self worthless, love useless.

In the month of July 2011, I spent nine days in medical hospitals and six days in detox (I went back to rehab instead of sleeping on the streets one night). I was arrested once and spent six days incarcerated. A place I had never been, never imagined, and never wanted to return to. The other ten days of the month, I was involved in a series of invasive, illegal crimes. The community was now on the look-out for me and my NA friend, my crime partner. Surveillance had me on tape and my DNA (I had open, bleeding wounds) and fingerprints were at most of the crime scenes. The news broadcasted the video and the papers ran pictures. We were wanted. Wanted! I was getting more paranoid and terrified by the day. Part of it was cocaine induced, but part of it was reality. This was not going to end well. How could we not be caught? Yet I didn't want to live, didn't care if I died, so nothing really mattered to me. All I could do was shoot cocaine—at any and all cost.

It was the early morning hours of August 4, 2011, when it all ended. Everything came to an abrupt halt. We had committed a crime earlier that night but had already run out of money and drugs. Therefore, my crime partner and I headed back out into the darkness of the night to commit another crime and get more drugs. Only this time, the police had beat us to the scene. Staked out in unidentified cars, they waited until the crime was in progress, at which point they rushed in, guns drawn, for the arrest. We were done; both of us headed to jail. They had us linked with all the other previous crimes. Whether I wanted to or not, whether I liked it or not, I was about to get clean—through metal handcuffs and the brute force of police detectives. Eight days after leaving my previous incarceration, I was heading back to jail. Only this time, a million dollar bail ensured that I was not leaving anytime soon.

PART IV

Incarceration

Back to the Basics

It took quite a while for me to clear up. I slept for the first week, getting up only to eat. I had no desire, motivation, or will to live, breath, or do anything. While in addiction, I had entirely forgotten your basic hygiene rules and it took a week for me to take my first shower. With two months in, I was showering every two to three days. It wasn't until about ninety days of incarceration and being clean that I began to shower again on a daily basis. It was a month before I brushed my teeth even once a day and again about ninety days until I could brush multiple times daily. I could not read or write coherently. Plus, journaling and books were a trigger for me. While on cocaine, I would read books and take notes incessantly. Writing guilt-ridden goodbye letters to Laila, poems to my mom, resolutions and plans for change. It was around thirty days clean when I picked up a book and began to read again. At ninety days, at the suggestion of my mother, I started a daily journal. I suffered from bruxism (an unconscious grinding of the teeth) and jaw popping for about two months, as my body slowly cleared up from the massive cocaine usage. I also ate—as much as possible and as often as possible—for the first two months. I put on the final, additional ten pounds—now having gained close to sixty pounds within less than a year's time. I felt and looked horrendous—honestly and literally—unrecognizable. As I began to become human again, many changes, subtle and distinct, were occurring on many levels. My mother started taking my collect calls, and we began to talk daily over the phone—a seemingly minor yet quite substantial key factor in my growth. Knowing I was going to remain incarcerated at least through the outcome of my trial, some vital, sanity-saving and humanity-building routines were set in place by my family. I called my mom daily and Laila took my call every other day. They both came up to visit me every Sunday afternoon. My dad visited every other Wednesday. These small routines often held me together, mentally and emotionally, and formed a stabilizing support structure on which I could rely and depend on as I began the daunting challenge of finding myself, finding recovery, and finding life once again.

I should make it known and very clear that I was fully convinced that I did not "want" to get clean. I know today that I honestly did but could not do so. In order to justify this incongruence, I had forced myself to believe that I didn't want to stop. It was easier than believing I was a worthless failure that couldn't stop. I had lost myself so deeply in addiction that all I had left of me was an obsessive, compulsive nature. It consumed me. The only qualities I recognized in myself were addiction's tendencies: conning, lying, stealing, and manipulating. The only behavior I exhibited was geared and guided and controlled by addiction: robbing, using, and getting more drugs. I identified myself with addiction because that is what consumed my entire being: a deep, total selfishness to get more at any cost. Naturally, it is uncharacteristic of addicts to stop, end, moderate, finish, complete, or be done with something—with anything, with everything. Nothing is ever enough, there cannot ever be enough, and it is an utter impossibility that I could, can, or will ever obtain enough. There is simply not enough. Ever. I was never going to wake up and "want" to stop, suddenly quit shooting coke, return to NA, and begin recovering again. That moment, that time, day, morning, etc., was never going to occur. I was never going to "want" to get clean, for I was far too consumed with addiction and like I indicated, addiction knows no end.

I also realized that I was never going to "feel" like getting clean either. I was waiting, waiting, waiting, for the day I would wake up and suddenly "feel" like recovering. That was not going to happen. I absolutely clung to that "borderline experience" and was desperately attached to the injection. The "feeling" of using—the rituals and the high—will always surpass a momentary desire, thought, or inkling about getting clean. Again, I was too far gone, too lost in addiction, too overtaken by the stronghold of late stage cocaine injecting, that any "feeling" I may have to stop using was quickly overpowered by the intensity of the compulsion to use.

But now I faced a predicament: everything I had ever done in my entire life had been based on what I wanted to do or what I felt like doing. Was there any other way to make a decision or any other principles by which to guide my life? I didn't know of any. Rebellion ran deep and discipline was foreign to me. Could I really do something because I "had" to do it? Even NA reinforced this with a slogan: Recovery is for people who want it, not for people who need it. I felt stuck. I didn't want to be clean, didn't feel like getting clean, yet I desperately needed to be clean. How was one to proceed? It was a powerful, revolutionary process as I came to an entirely new level of thinking: *I had to get clean.* No choice involved, no questions asked, no feelings acknowledged. Detectives, shackles and handcuffs, and incarceration told me: "You are getting clean." Forced now to be clean, I had my first truly empowering choice: How would I respond to this enforced recovery?

Growing up, I wanted nothing to do with discipline, as seen by my rebellious behavior at the age of thirteen. I was dating my first boyfriend when my mom tried to prohibit our time together, restrict my social activities, and limit my freedom. I forcefully and aggressively refused to be told no. I had never developed a vital, valuable living skill necessary for successful navigation of the grown-up world. It was in jail, where this principle of discipline became deeply engrained and became a reality for me. I likened it to my kindergarten experience. I screamed, cried, kicked, and threw massive temper tantrums on the step of my classroom every morning until my parents finally transferred me to a different school. This was a pivotal opportunity to learn discipline, and I thoroughly began to understand the numerous layers involved in that single incident. I was being taken from my daily five-year-old routine of playing, running, being outdoors. I now had to get up early, get dressed and ready, and spend the day in school. No way! I wanted nothing to do with this sudden change! Yet this is precisely the importance of learning discipline. At five years old, no one was going to ask me if I "wanted" to go to kindergarten—I would have said no! I wanted to play all day. No one asked me how I "felt" about going to kindergarten, as if that were supposed to impact my participation. I would have responded that I felt horrible, angry, upset, and miserable about this school thing. No, no one asks a five-year-old those things because they do not matter: *I had to go.* Like it or not, feel like it or not, want to not… I was going to school. Decision made. Case closed. No choice. Here is where the personal choice does lie: not in whether or not I am going to kindergarten— that was decided for me, I'm going. Rather, my freedom of choice lies in how I choose to respond to it. I accept the discipline and choose my response. I could cry, whine, complain, and be miserable. I might get a few teachers to feel bad for me, maybe out of pity or sympathy give me a few hugs or a lollipop. That's one option: misery. I could respond by being miserable about the decision.

Or… I could choose a second alternative: a cheerful smile and a joyful heart with a spirit of open-mindedness. Maybe then, I just might learn something. Instead of remaining distracted by anger, hostility, and resentment because I could not get "my way," I could embark on the journey ahead with a sense of discovery and fascination. Now the value of paying attention, being focused, and listening and learning in kindergarten is obvious: one learns the basic, fundamentals of successful living! Had I been intent of creating self-pity throughout my kindergarten experience, I would have missed invaluable, substantial life lessons. Like the ABCs—the foundation of communication and relating to the world. I would have missed lessons like sharing and counting and colors and shapes. The essential building blocks of life are learned in kindergarten and my personal choice of responding determines my success. Will I learn the vital foundational tools to successfully navigate my way through the rest of my educational years? Or will I leave kindergarten lacking these necessary and important skills? The answer lies in my response to the situation. Will I embrace this newfound adventure or resist this sudden, possibly uncomfortable life change?

When I had that "kindergarten vision" and subsequent realizations, it marked a significant and drastic change in my attitude, view, and perception of recovery. I was incarcerated, being forced to get clean. My empowerment was in how I responded to my present difficult situation: would I welcomely embrace recovery or reject this opportunity for growth? For the first time, possibly ever, I made a direct, intentional, personal choice: I decided to wholeheartedly accept this valuable time for growth, development, and change. I was going to earnestly and fervently seek recovery, as only the dying can. For as long as I can remember, I had been caught up by some form of obsession or addiction at some level. At worse, debilitatingly consumed by it; at best, selfishly distracted. It took many forms throughout my life: food, weight, men, drugs, success, status, money, education, self-improvement, etc. Self, self, self. It was always about me. An addiction always hindered my ability to freely choose by distorting my intentions and clouding out reasoning. Rational, logical thinking was impossible because of a constant, relentless need to fix, change, manage, control, or otherwise alter myself or my life in some way, internal or external. Yet suddenly, through this remarkable understanding of the extraordinary concept of discipline, I now had the power of choice. The decision regarding the situation was not up to me: I was getting clean, like it or not. My power came from choosing to recover.

This was the first of many, frequent profound psychic changes that took place within my early days of incarceration. Nothing was ever going to make me "want" to get clean, not homelessness, not crime, not short-term jail stays, not unemployment, nor neglect of my own child. Not loss of respect nor loss of family concern or involvement. Not having to lie, steal, cheat, scheme, and manipulate my way through life. Not financial bankruptcy or massive credit debt. Not shame or embarrassment. Not even my mother preparing for her own daughter's funeral. I had crossed a line and there was now no consequence too great. I was never going to "want" to get clean, but I saw the possibility that if I were forced to be clean and decided to choose to recover, I may possibly one day want to stay that way. It was worth a shot. I would give it my all—my thoughts, feelings, words, and actions. I would devote all my time, effort, and involvement into recovery. I would give recovery my full and undivided attention. If I was making my first real intentional choice, I was going to pursue it passionately and eagerly. My life was on the line: recover or die is an accurate scale, given the way I use drugs. I knew I could not walk out of jail the same person I walked in as or I would go right back to doing what I always did, what I knew, my default personality: addiction.

Now that I had made a commitment to recovery, things had to change. I knew from previous experience, the steps were the solution, so onto the steps I went. I was having some difficulty in picking a fellowship, however. Not that I needed to decide immediately—I was in jail and both NA and AA meetings were brought to me. AA came three times a week and NA once. I started going through the steps by mail with an NA sponsor, one of the women who brought the meeting in on Monday nights. That relationship didn't work and I was really starting to enjoy and relate to the women from AA. Plus, I still held some minor to major resentments with the people of NA, as a fellowship and with certain individuals. My upset with NA (people, not the program) came from my feeling abandoned. I had spent over twelve years of my life having grown up in that fellowship, yet when it came time to help a member in need, no one showed up. None of my long-term NA friends wrote to me or reached out to my mom or daughter while I was incarcerated. I was angry and hurt. I contrasted this with the commitment to service displayed among AA members. The AA responsibility statement—being available whenever anyone reaches out for help—is part of an engrained, vital purpose in AA. I admired their no-nonsense approach to the necessities of the program: meetings, steps, sponsorship, and above all else, service to the newcomer. I also greatly admired the step process in AA: direct, forefront, prompt, immediate. It was time for me to get down to business. I wrote a fourth step and an AA member came up to the jail and did a fifth step with me. I was able to go through all the steps, except the ninth step—making amends—because a big part of amends is a change in behavior. I needed to be out of jail, living, working, and breathing this new way of life before I could properly show people that I had changed, that things were indeed different. This could not be done by a jailhouse letter from an inmate but would have to wait until my re-entry into society where I could best prove my new-found nature. It would be necessary—imperative, actually, to obtain a sponsor and go through the steps after my release. This initial step work was necessary because the pain, guilt, remorse, and shame was so pressing and overwhelming—there was an urgent demand to cleanse, trust, and discover. But the real world would entail all sorts of new challenges and difficulties, activities and relationships, responsibilities and commitments, dreams and goals. Once back in the community, it would be important that I connect with a strong sponsor and develop a relationship with her through step work.

I have since let go of my anger with NA: addicts are human too and I had barely even been involved with the fellowship for many years. It also could have been my own lack of a twelfth step that I saw in others. I had never formally or thoroughly worked a twelfth step and this lack thereof was now my current complaint with the fellowship. The first time I was on a twelfth step, I changed sponsors and started the steps over again, beginning at step one. The second time I arrived at step 12, I left NA. I was unwilling to integrate into my life two of the vital concepts of this step. First, practicing these principles in all my affairs. I had relapsed into bulimia and did not want to face it. Instead of "sharing clean and living dirty," I left NA, had stopped going to meetings, and sunk further into dishonesty. Second, carrying the message. When it came time for me to pass it onto others, I saw no point. Instead of giving back, I left NA, with the erroneous arrogance that it had nothing more to teach me. Even if that was somehow the case, as a recovering addict, I had an obliga-tion, a personal responsibility to pass it onto others. To give freely all that I had been given. Neglecting and disinterested in the newcomer, I left NA—to my own and many others destruction.

This apparent lack of selflessness that appeared in NA could very well have been because I had never developed it within myself. Through working the steps in jail, I realized my utter selfishness and was able to forgive myself for this devastating mistake. It was then that I was able to stop blaming NA and take responsibility for meeting my recovery needs. Whether AA or NA, it is certain that I need a supportive, recovering community to depend on and rely upon for personal growth.

Spiritual Transformation

The first month in jail was extremely painful: terror, anxiety, guilt, depression, fear. Shame consumed me. I was detoxing from a horrendous, brutal relapse and my mind and feelings were reawakening. I was overcome with agony and regret. Deep painful memories haunted me continuously. Desire and obsession to use plagued me constantly. I would lay in bed, alone, cold, and full of fear. All I could think about was the horrible mess I was in and what was going to happen to me. I needed a way out of the insanity of my own mind. I needed God.

There was no longer a "convenient" way to recover—meetings were sporadic, sponsorship largely unavailable, reach out calls nearly impossible. To make it even more difficult, I was not in an environment conducive to recovery. The drug talk was incessant, gossip and slander rampant, stealing prevalent. There was fighting frequently, as I was in a hostile atmosphere. I learned something called the criminal code, an entirely immoral, backward code of unspoken rules and ways of living. This was really hard on me, as I did not understand this, could not identify with it, and often got it wrong. The criminal code's most hurtful guideline for me was the way no one wants anything good to happen to anyone else. This lack of a supportive, encouraging environment was foreign to me and I did not have an easy time with this new way of relating to my peers. The hardest thing about being incarcerated was, for me, not having a community of like-minded individuals to turn to for help, love, and support. People who uplift and inspire each other; people who want the best for each other. Jail taught me a whole new and different lifestyle— one of jealousy, greed, and backstabbing. Dog eat dog. Every woman for herself. Little kindness, even less respect, and no unconditional love. It was difficult.

Then, about thirty days into my stay, something extraordinary occurred. I take this directly from a journal entry I wrote that night:

Sunday, September 4, 2011

"A magical transformation took place within me tonight. No doubt about it, God reached out and touched a suffering soul, lifting my spirits and healing my heart in a profound and beautiful way: forgiveness.

What an astonishing *gift*. What a beautiful *grace*. What a tremendous and powerful change. What a remarkable God. Inspiration and light, peace and hope, a positive outlook on the future—all these feelings, these immense gifts given to me just now by a God who excitedly awaited this moment: my redemption. My personal salvation. The moment in time when the past would be healed, all is forgiven, and the opportunity arises to move on. Spiritual insight reigns supreme and the devil stands no chance at this moment. Yes, this is my moment, my *gracious (grace-given) gift* from an unconditional God— this is my moment in time. My soul sought frantically, relentlessly, for this moment. And here it exists. Here I relish in the complete comfort of God's forgiveness. Which is ultimately, self-forgiveness. Letting go of the horrendous burdens of guilt, regret, and shame, all of which had become my constant companions. Insert now joy, peace, renewal—an inherent recognition—a nostalgic familiarity. Yes, here within lies absolute wholeness: *I am love.*"

In full gratitude and contentment, Sara

Yes, it was that remarkable. Yes, it was that life-altering, profound, and cleansing. Even writing now, I can vividly recall the evening. I was reading Ekhart Tolle's book *The Power of Now*, and I became overwhelmed with the flood of spiritual insight that engulfed me. I closed my eyes for a quiet meditation and saw visions of fields— each blade of grass vividly, perfectly designed. I could see the dew drops on every leaf and petal. It was pure beauty. Looking back, I had searched my whole life for that moment, never really knowing or believing it could or did even exist. A moment where my spirit was completely transformed, forgiveness and grace showered upon me, and I knew God.

I slept at no time during the night and I didn't even want to. I was enamored, captivated by my newfound existence; this amazing thought process that I was unfamiliar with, the wisdom and insight that now pervaded my mind, the absolute peace and serenity regarding what the future held, and most clearly of all: the full and complete knowledge that I was God's beloved child.

As quickly as my life spiraled downward in addiction, after this experience, multiply the rate of recovery by 100 and that is how quickly and often new, higher revelations and teachings were being given to me. It was tremendous.

My mother went through this process with me. Our daily phone call was vital—my lifeline—to well-being. Having the faith of a saint, she became my rock—my loyal confidant in this intense period of renewal. Talking to my mom every day and Laila every other day held me together—giving me something to enjoy in life and a connection to the real world.

There were many incredible insights; the early ones struck me powerfully, as I was not used to receiving such a high level of knowledge. Spiritual theories were becoming my reality. The God I had always known to be "out there" was now personal, close, and intimate to me. I finally had access to the astounding power and strength of God. Although I had always known of it intellectually (I knew God was there and believed God was available to help), I had never before been able to utilize or access this divine power. Concepts of God became reality for me.

Some of the many life-changing insights:

o   Good things do not happen because I am who I am; rather, good things happen because God is who God is:

There is no more "striving" for perfection, there's nothing to "achieve" that I don't already have! This insight completely eliminated my drive for power, success, and accomplishment. The "good girl" image was gone—being good wasn't what earned me anything! God didn't bestow grace upon me because I was good—quite the opposite! God's love comes freely, unmerited, unwarranted, uncalled for, and completely undeserved. There is nothing I can do to get it, work for it, or strive to achieve it. God loves me simply because God loves me.

o   Feelings vs. States of Being:

This difference became crystal clear to me. The nature of feelings is transient, comes and goes quickly, unexpectedly—often in response to thoughts and situations. Feelings can be acknowledged, but they are just as unimportant as any random thought that occurs in my mind. Feelings give a barometer to my reactions and should be allowed to pass through the being without much attention. The place to reside is in the states of being—which are unchanging, eternal, always present, and readily available. This ability to select a state of being at any given time suddenly became open to me.

Divine principles became ways of living—a moral code of conduct previously unknown to me. I watched as regardless of my external conditions—which were violent, degrading, and often oppositional—I held on to an innate, inherent state of joy, dignity, integrity, and honor. There was nothing in my circumstances that could have "caused" these principles to arise within me—they were simply there because they belong to me and are who I am. Nothing or no one could take it or shake it. Joy and gratitude overflowed my heart—for no reason! On the outside, I looked and saw white and gray, concrete and metal. Yet on the inside, I felt a solace and comfort in God. Peace radiated from me and a gentle calmness emulated from my demeanor.

Some things began to change naturally for me: I could no longer participate in drug talk or gossip; it became inappropriate for me to engage in certain behaviors, like stealing, lying, overeating, or purging. I had carried all these behaviors into jail with me and now they were not okay. Remarkably, I found the willingness and strength, through this newfound connection with God, to stop, end, and change all old behaviors. Everything about me became new. I felt, acted, spoke, and thought like an entirely new creation. It was a steady progress of letting go more and more of all the unnecessary and counterproductive habits and behaviors. I found that I knew what to eliminate by what blocked me from God. More and more of me began to diminish, being replaced by the principles and character of God.

These wondrous changes—this spiritual purification—that was occurring within me was incredible, empowering, and inspiring. It was clear to me that I had nothing to do with what was happening to me, aside from the fact that I was agreeing to the help and participating in receiving awareness. I knew I had been selected, found by God. I also knew this was either (a) the reason for my coming to jail or (b) happening because I was in jail. Whatever the case, practically daily I was being swept away by a divine force sent for renewal and cleansing. I wanted to know more of who this God was.

My academic search for God did not begin in jail. It had been an ongoing struggle for many years, since I was a teenager. I had always known there was something "wrong" with me and I figured God could "fix" it. So off I went from an early age, in a relentless pursuit for truth. Only now, here in jail, it was much different: God had found me. I went into the library and began to read every spiritual, theological, philosophical, God-directed book. I started off with inspirational, hope-filled messages and slowly found my way to scholarly material. I wanted truth—not hearsay or opinion—I was looking for moral dogma. I found myself immersed in my childhood God of Christianity.

One afternoon, I was reading a book by a Buddhist monk and I knew, plain and clear, that this was not for me. I was no longer looking to be cured, fixed, or saved. I wanted to pick my faith according to the God who had called me. Having studied Buddhism in years previous, I was now able to say no with valid and relevant explanations. First, Buddhism has no "God" and I was abundantly clear that a higher, divine source had been connecting with me, working through me, and transforming all of me. Second, the Buddhists have no formal concept of prayer—since there is no authority or higher power to pray to. This was key for me—I lived in prayer, relied on prayer, and trusted in prayer. If I was going to pick a personal religion, prayer had to be a component of it. Third, suffering is the core philosophy of Buddhism—there is no hope. I could not connect myself with a way of life whose entire premise was based on the idea of suffering. Therefore, the main three tenets I was searching for in a religion: God, communication and relationship with that God, and hope and inspiration for the future—these were entirely absent in Buddhism. I put the book down and in that moment, I chose Christianity.

I attended all the Bible studies and church services held frequently throughout the week. One particular night, a minister proposed the "ten-day challenge." It involved simply reading the Bible and praying attentively every single day for ten days in a row. I love a good challenge and this minister claimed that remarkable things would follow for those who embarked upon it. I was sitting in jail, in desperate need of a miracle for release and this guy was promising remarkable things. I was sold.

I had read the gospels during college in a religious studies class and had been taught all the skepticism and criticism regarding Jesus, the compilation of the New Testament, the corruption of His teachings, the time frame it was written, etc. Everything added up to me back then: the Bible was man-made, misconstrued, and Jesus was a great prophet, exhibiting the full potential of humanity. Somebody we should strive to emulate. Certainly, I was a Jesus fan, but the Son of God? Well, probably not.

I picked up my Bible on Monday, October 17, 2011, the day after the church service. I didn't stop reading until I had absorbed every word of that powerful book. I was astounded. Shocked. Utterly amazed. Enthralled. Captivated. It was recommended I start with John's Gospel, then read the New Testament, then go onto the Old Testament. I read the Bible in its entirety in twenty-two days. I could not put it down. Ironically, during that time, my drug and alcohol counselor was out for two weeks, leaving me free to read for six or eight hours a day. I loved every second of my reading, mesmerized by the stories, teachings, and the authors. Paul was absolutely my favorite author. Some books of the Old Testament were hard to get through—the constant warfare and destruction or the tedious details regarding materials for the ark of the covenant, or the hundreds of names of ancestors listed in the descendants sections. But I got through it and I found a remarkable God: an interactive, personal, merciful God. The kind of God I needed for a miracle. My mom heard daily of my Bible learnings and we shared many insights and understandings together. I hadn't yet convinced myself through and through that Jesus was God and I wasn't yet interested in returning to my Catholic roots but I had made a tremendous start: I believed in the God of the Bible.

At this time, I requested a Christian mentor. All but a few of the services held at the jail were given by Bible-based, nondenominational Christian ministries. This was just what I needed at the time—they were filled with hope and spirit and joy. I felt uplifted, connected, and inspired after their services. However, I began to notice that some important pieces were missing in these nondenominational faiths. I needed Mary, the mother of God, as part of my faith. I also needed the sacraments I had received and learned in grade school. I began to crave a solemn, reverent mass so I began attending the Catholic church service every Wednesday night. I had returned to my childhood faith. I decided if I was truly going to be a Catholic, I wanted a full understanding of my religion—dogma, traditions, beliefs, everything. I requested a Catholic mentor and she gave me a few books. One was about intercessory prayer and the other was the Catechism of the Catholic Church. I loved it—I absorbed its every teaching. It's mainly a reference book, written and read like a college textbook, but I found it to be exactly what I was looking for. As a scholar, I wanted facts, knowledge, and truth. In the Catechism, I found every facet of my rediscovered faith. I was sold. I became a recommitted Catholic.

Books were my main teachers and sole friends while incarcerated. It's said that the reader rises to the level of the consciousness of the author, similarly as if engaging in direct conversation. I decided I was only going to give my attention to inspirational material that would uplift, support, and encourage me on my newfound journey into recovery. I refused to read violent, hateful, trashy, vulgar, or criminal books. I would not allow myself to be lowered to that level of thinking. Plus, true crime and mystery novels scare me and always have. I watched the movie *The Ring* in 2004 and still have nightmares if I think about that girl's face in the mirror. Ugh. I'm a sensitive soul. So I carefully selected my authors: who did I want to speak with? What type of language did I want to engage in? I loved reading. I often thought that I could have earned a degree from BCCF's library. We went to library twice a week and were allowed to take out three books at a time. I read autobiographies of extraordinary people, biographies of great historical figures, and every Christian book on the shelf. I stayed away from self-help but found a few new-age authors to be amazingly inspirational. At first, that was mostly what I was looking for: to be inspired, encouraged, and given hope during my dark, desperate situation. I needed a miracle and set out to find every reason why I should/could/can receive one. The results were incredible—I found insightful, hopeful writers sharing a touching message. They were my friends. Eventually, when I discovered joy for myself,

I began to seek educational authors. I am an academic at heart, true scholar through and through: inquisitive, skeptical without proof, and hungry for answers. But incidentally enough, I am also convinced of spiritual influence, drawn to wisdom and understanding in a mystical sense, with an uncanny ability to perceive subtle underpinnings. I see spiritual purpose, meaning, and principles everywhere and in all things. Early on, during the intense period of spiritual revelation, I was given divine precepts and an extensive collection of divine principles by which to live. True spiritual principles are never in conflict and this distinction became clear to me as I learned to practice these newfound guidelines in my life in jail. It had always been known to me that I could not leave jail the same person I was when I came in and *now* is the time to change—not when I get out. If I could not learn to live in integrity, honesty, dignity, and honor while in jail, I stood no chance of succeeding in the real world.

Divine Precepts

I had started a meditation practice while incarcerated. I would sit in silent meditation for forty minutes at night and forty minutes in the morning. During one of these quiet sessions, I was given six basic divine precepts—goals or guidelines by which to live. They have helped me tremendously in daily difficulties or when facing challenges. I could, and possibly may, write an entire book on these principles alone. Here is a brief description of each six factors:

1. Mental Discipline: clear discernment (the ability to decipher God-given thoughts versus negative thinking), ability to choose where the attention is placed, guarding one's well-being as if protecting a precious gem, being careful of what one is being exposed to—conversations I participate in and listen to, words I speak, TV and movies I watch, people I place myself around

2. Moral Perfection: impeccable integrity, doing the right thing at the right time all the time, fine-tuning one's intuition, creating a clear channel for my conscience, listening to that still, quiet voice within. Now matter how inconsequential or trivial, always being my word, doing what is right and in alignment with my true self, which is God's will for my life

3. Spiritual Enlightenment: being fully present in the *now*, taking full responsibility for the moment, letting go of the past and trusting in the future (of which neither exist), expressing the greatest joy and ability—the absolute unlimitedness of the now, expressing my divine birth right and human responsibility for creating, living, and being the greatness of God's child

4. Emotional Balance: reasoning over emotions, basing decisions on clear, rational thought, taking nothing personal, letting go of grudges, self-righteous anger, and justified resentments, fear, worry, and regret. Stepping back and pausing prior to acting, responding appropriately rather than reacting impulsively

5. Physical Well-Being: eat less, move more. Physical activity daily, keeping the body firm, lean, and agile, carefully selecting what fuels the body—choosing wholesome, lovingly grown and prepared foods, being sensitive to the body's responses and needs and cravings, listening to the messages and signals which the body will consistently send

6. Fun and Recreation: enjoyment and laughter, leisure and play

Priority Reorganization

*A*nother important factor that I needed to take a look at early in my recovery was evaluating and re-prioritizing my life. What was important to me, what I valued, and where I wanted to place my time and attention. When I arrived at jail, everything about me was addiction: every thought, word, feeling, action was geared toward a selfish angle. I was entirely grounded in self-centered pleasure, obsession, and excitement. I wanted to feel good constantly.

I quickly realized that in order to change, grow, and develop, everything about me must change. With the blessing of spiritual awareness, I watched in awe and wonder as inappropriate, immoral, and unacceptable parts of me began to fall away—with great ease and tremendous grace. Things I had never before been able to change, like bulimia, or patterns and ideas so deeply engrained, like total self-centeredness, suddenly and naturally diminished and then disappeared. I was amazed at the willingness I now had available to me to let go of any useless habit, old idea, erroneous belief, or maladaptive behavior. Some dropped away immediately, others reduced, then ultimately ended. Some pop up still occasionally and a sharpened, heightened conscience quickly calls for correction. Here are some of the things that I could no longer do or changes that began to develop:

About sixty days in, I realized it was best, given the environment I was living in, to speak only when spoken to. This small, simple change transformed my life. I lost all desire to gossip, to know of the happenings on the block or in others' trials. I would freely and kindly respond to anyone who approached me, but rarely did I engage in direct communication. I talked with my mother daily and to Laila, of course. This habit of speaking only when spoken to gave me observer insight. I spent hours of my day in prayer. It was not a commitment consciously made at first, instead I found this communication came naturally as I began to distance myself from the negativity behind the walls. I also lost all desire to eavesdrop on others' conversations. Of course, every opportunity I got to speak with a person from the outside, I took up enthusiastically. Normal, intelligent, soulful conversations would carry me for days—whether it was with my drug and alcohol counselor, my Catholic mentor, group facilitator, lawyer, or even the librarian. This human interaction sustained me during my period of isolation, which is largely why my mom and Laila's phone calls were so vitally important to me. I worked hard to not adapt or conform to the criminal code pervading this unique sub-culture in which I found myself residing. But this behavioral choice often required strenuous effort and deliberate action on my part and frequently excluded and isolated me from my inmate peers. As long as I had regular human contact on a personal level, which I did, I was willing to pay the price of seclusion.

I developed a rule for myself: do not put my hands on anything which does not belong to me. Along with this, I also took on another personal rule: no borrowing. It is better to give then to receive. If I didn't have it and could not obtain it through my own resources; I didn't need it. I had always been a taker in life. Takers take what doesn't belong to them, take more than they need, and desire to live off somebody else's dime. I no longer had the desire to take anything from anyone. Not even a piece of candy from my roommate or a pen from class. If I couldn't obtain it through my own resources, I didn't want it. This new level of honesty and integrity was amazing for me. I often shocked myself. After all, I had entered jail a thief, and as far as I can remember, had always had this characteristic about me.

I also began to exercise again. It had been almost two years since I had had any interest or involvement in a regular fitness routine. This forgotten hobby was rekindled about ninety days into my incarceration. I wanted to move! I wanted to work out. I had always had a passion for physical exercise, but addiction had diminished my motivation greatly. I had lost all desire to move or exercise, coupled with a raging eating disorder and gaining fifty pounds. To once again have the motivation and enthusiasm to exercise delighted me! It was also a clear sign to my mother that I was getting better: my old self was beginning to emerge and I was paying attention to my health and body again. As I continued to exercise daily, my mother's faith in my recovery was strengthened. She knew that I was horrified about being overweight and to see me taking corrective action and working toward slimness showered her that my spirit was returning. And it was. I exercised continuously, not obsessively, just extensively. The only form of exercise allowed in jail was walking. So I paced the block up and down for about three to four hours every day. I cut out TV time and replaced it with walking. I developed a routine of walking, forty-five minute sessions at a time, three to four times a day. It became valuable prayer time. I was doing my morning and evening formal meditation, but my time with God was now becoming close to constant. I found that cutting out television eliminated the mundaneness of early evening sitcom reruns. An added benefit of walking: it removed me from the negativity and created a positive experience. People began to notice my commitment and subsequent weight loss and a few of my peers attempted to join me in my walking routine. I felt more like myself than I had ever before in my entire life. Physical fitness is fun and important to me, but I gave it up for addiction. To have an enjoyable hobby back, with full commitment, passion, and motivation, revealed to me that change truly was occurring.

I gave up all excess food. This change alone could equate to an entire book. I have historically always craved food more than cocaine, at least until the end of my using. Food addiction has been with me since childhood. I barely knew a life without food obsession and an intense desire to eat. To have this addiction relieved was so extraordinary to me, actually, it felt unbelievable. I can only credit it to God. I literally began to fall in love with the process of learning and coming to know and understand Jesus. I cannot even describe it—the process was magical, joyful, and intimate. Here's where the true inner healing took place—I had a sudden, deep urge to give something of myself to Jesus. I wanted to tangibly, physically offer my newfound love to my Lord and Savior. Previously, I would have laughed at and shunned you if you would have tried to tell me "Jesus heals" or "Jesus saves." I would have given you no mind at all. A spiritual transformation was the last thing on this planet I thought would happen to me.

But it did. Undeniably, unexpectedly, wholeheartedly. Since I could not physically give anything to Jesus Himself, I began to wonder instead what I could give up for him. I had read in the Bible that fasting enhanced prayer and I had a major prayer request. So I meditated on the concept and an idea came to me. To show Jesus how much I loved Him, I would give up something I desperately loved: food. I began immediately. I gave all of my sweets and desserts away at meals. I ended all commissary orders. I did not eat in between meals and I did not eat food from anyone else's tray (this is a common disgusting occurrence in chow hall). Then I wanted to do more, so I gave up as much as I could at every meal, usually about half of my tray. Other female inmates began to purposefully sit near me because they knew I gave up most of my food.

I used to lay in bed at night, deeply craving food. For as long as I can remember, I had always been severely and dysfunctionally attached to food. Especially when the drugs were gone. Rehabs were where I had gained almost all of my excess weight. Take the drugs away from me and food becomes my new best friend. But this magical and inspiring new mind-set I suddenly had surrounding food floored me. It astonished and amazed me. I could not believe that me—a raging bulimic—could love anything more than food and eating. Yet here I was, giving it all up to show Jesus my heart. Who would have ever thought this was possible? Certainly not I. Over nine inpatient hospitalizations, more than ten years of sporadic therapy, even involvement in the OA fellowship. Nothing was able to ultimately resolve my lifelong struggle with food addiction. Until I landed in jail with a deep, real, sincere, and heartfelt prayer request. Suddenly, nothing was more important than being close to Jesus. All along, Jesus had been my answer. Doing for me what I could not do for myself, relieving me of the food obsession.

These behavioral changes were just a few of the major differences between my old and new way of thinking. A lot had to do with me clearing out personally and inwardly on every dimension. There were dramatic changes, necessary and beneficial.

- Physically—I began exercising and eating much less, thereby healthy weight loss ensued.
- Emotionally—previously unknown to me before, there was a sincere understanding and relatedness to others.
- Spiritually—I practiced meditation, listened to my intuition, prayed unceasingly, and I saw God everywhere.
- Mentally—I was more alert, aware, and concise than ever. I learned to redirect my thoughts automatically when needed.

Now clear, available and open, I could effectively evaluate my life. What is important to me? What truly matters? What do I most value? In asking myself these questions, I had to admit, I have been way off target my entire life, always operating with an inner selfishness in me. In fact I realized I didn't take the time to ever truly, honestly, intimately get to know a single other person—or did I ever care to. There was always a distracting addiction preventing me from being fully sincere, selfless, considerate of others, or loving. In fact, for many, many years I secretly harbored the belief that I was incapable of love. I didn't feel it, know it, have it, show it, or experience it. One form of addiction or another always blocked my ability not only to give of myself to the fullest degree, but also to understand you enough to relate. And that is what, in my evaluation of life's meaning, became highly important. Relationship and connection with others. Not socially or superficially, as I would an acquaintance. But relating in a way that requires full and complete disclosure, often without spoken words—and openness to all that you are, were, could be, and will be. Being with someone eye to eye, sincerely and intensely. Relationship that requires sincerity, time, love, and attention. Addiction robs individuals of these four indispensable qualities. It corrupts and perverts intentions and destroys value and meaning. True, lasting, real connection cannot exist without these four characteristics:

- Sincerity: approaching every relationship with an honest, invested interest in who you are. Making a very real, genuine effort to understand you as a unique person.
- Time: dedicating what we treasure the most—our time. Giving of it freely, often, and joyfully.
- Love: unconditionally, nonjudgmentally offering my compassionate support to you. Creating the space for you to be your absolute best around me.
- Attention: giving you my undivided, focused concentration, remembering what you say, learning things you do, understanding how you think and feel, coming to know what's important to you.

Relationships became a priority to me—a brand-new, unknown important facet of my life. The people who loved and supported me through incarceration showed me the value of true friendship. These people I wanted to have in my life—often, regularly, and frequently. My aunts and uncles, siblings and cousins, and other long-term friends. I now wanted to be there for them. I strongly desired to get to know them, to share a sense of love and belonging with others.

The most painful relationship to face was with my Laila. It had been about two years since I have truly been her mother—as in, there for her, responsible for her, and committed to her. Seeing my long-standing selfishness in regards to Laila made me cringe in horror, shame, and regret. I now had a thirteen-year-old, amazing little girl that I barely knew inside. Rebuilding our relationship became a top priority to me. Above all else, Laila deserved me now. My needs, wants, desires, interests, and addictions always took precedence over raising my own daughter. I didn't have the time to pay attention to her needs, desires, hopes, and dreams. To learn about her personal talents, strengths, joys, and loves. These kind of things became my new favorite interest. Learning about her emotional needs became number one in my life. Spending the time it takes to get to know her deeply and fully and wholly became most important to me. Bringing out her highest dreams, encouraging her personal goals, discovering her unique talents became my sole purpose for living. Having been thoroughly self-absorbed, I had been thoroughly unavailable to my own daughter. In re-prioritizing, Laila became my main interest again. This was my child and as she entered her teenage years, I had a responsibility to be present and available to her. I have a moral and physical obligation to be mature and focused so as to guide her wisely. To teach her strong values and judgment and wholesome decision-making skills. To learn about her friendships and who my daughter is on the inside. Finally (although about time I grew up), Laila had become important to me.

I also knew that recovery had to be a priority and that it was a lifelong commitment. I was joyfully okay with that. I can always learn, always grow, always develop and mature. But even more so, there is a message of freedom to be carried. There are people coming into recovery after me, hopeless and broken and lost, just as I was. Some worse, some not quite as bad, but all striving for a change, all desperate for a new way of life. I need to be that hope. With step work empowering me, those beginning on this journey can benefit from my experience, strength, and hope only if I remain active and available in recovery. It's not all about me—it actually never was and never will be. The only difference is, that now I recognize that.

Deterrents to Relapse

After such a brutal, savage active addiction, why would I ever want to return to a life like that after I had experienced the freedom brought on by recovery? Understanding of the nature of addiction, I knew better than to assume that I was in the free and clear. Hardly so. Everything about me screamed addiction—the lifestyle consumed me. There were no areas of my life that using had not taken over. Addiction had invaded and captured my entire being. I was held hostage by a dark, powerful, captivating disease. Addiction enslaved me for so long and so completely, that I no longer cared if I was in chains. Bondage was all I knew. Freedom existed somewhere, at sometime, for some people, but it came nowhere near me. I was lost, hopeless, and broken—again. Only this time, the consequences were much more severe, widespread, and damaging.

Since addiction so thoroughly pervaded my entire life and being, everything was a trigger to me. The cravings were intense and absolutely relentless. I began to start a mental task of redirecting my thoughts whenever I found my mind turning to drugs—which was about every forty seconds. It was painful, difficult, and exhausting. I would sit down to watch television and the people next to me would be discussing the hottest corners in Philly to cop drugs on. Time to redirect. I would be at the chow hall dinner table and the conversation across from me would be about the fun of overdosing. Redirect.

I'd be in the dispensary and the nurse would be drawing blood from another inmate. Redirect. I'd be walking outside during yard and the girls would be fighting over shooting versus smoking cocaine. Redirect. And the list goes on and on and on. I was living with 100-plus inmates, 97 percent of whom were drug addicts. It was not an easy environment in which to get clean. It was even harder to recover.

I often envisioned myself as a turtle. When interaction with the other girls was unavoidable, I would tuck myself away into my protective shell. It was my safety precaution, my way of protecting myself from the harmful and dangerous habit of glorifying addiction. Bruce, my phenomenal drug and alcohol counselor, taught me about euphoric recall. I called it drug nostalgia. Same thing. It's when I daydream about using, or reminisce about the lifestyle or glorify the crimes of addiction to the point where I am back in that time full force. For someone like me, with an intense and powerful addiction, these flashback memories are fatal. I could not afford even moments of recollection of the once so-called pleasure of using drugs. I knew and held on to tightly the fact that all cravings will eventually fade, pass, then disappear. As I distance myself further from addiction, while simultaneously drawing myself deeper into recovery, the incessant stronghold of using loosens its grip. As I focus more on staying clean, I found I was spending less time constantly redirecting my thoughts. The urges were diminishing in strength and frequency, but they still seemed to appear all the time. I was willing to hold on and wait for the miracle because I knew that at some point, I would lose the desire and obsession to shoot cocaine. Even if it stayed with me for two years, even if the idea of using again seemed attractive to me for a decade—I truly believed and knew from experience that I would one day no longer think about or want that kind of life or that substance. So I held on.

I prayed faithfully for two things regarding cravings:

1. I asked God to please remove all desire and obsession to use.
2. I asked God to instill within me a natural, intense repulsion to shooting drugs.

Day in and day out, I repeated my requests, especially when the urges came.

It requires a special kind of creativity to truly recover in jail. I frequently found myself in places where I could not remove myself from danger situations. I couldn't walk out of the group if the conversation turned to needle injection. I wasn't allowed to leave the dining room or return in from the yard if the talk was triggering me. I had to get creative because staying away from people, places, and things is vital to remaining clean and I was living in a place surrounded by people, who discussed things that I could not participate in. I began to hold my ears closed and sing to myself. Nursery rhymes and Jesus songs played over and over in my head to protect me from going down a bad road in my thinking. I didn't have the luxury of getting clean on the outside, where meetings are held at all times of the day, where a call to a sponsor is as easy as picking up the phone or where a supportive friend is only a drive away.

When obsessions got too bad or they would persist for a few days, Bruce would remind me to write a "Pros and Cons" list and a "Benefits of Recovery" list. Then he would instruct me to read and reread the cons, allowing them to sink deep into my heart so I could truly feel the consequences. There were two powerful "pros" to shooting cocaine for me:

1. I had a vicious needle addiction.
2. The borderline overdose experience

There were three substantial and meaningful "cons":

1. My mother: we had built such a bond through our daily phone call. She held me together through everything. She never gave up on me. She believed in me when no one else did, she truly supported me, and she was the only one left when there was no one else. My mother. I knew she enjoyed having her Sara back. I knew she smiled when she spoke of me now. Not because she knew that I was "safe in jail"—but because I was her friend again. This relationship

meant so much to me. I wanted to do nothing that would ever disappoint my mother again.

2. My Laila: I could sense that I was walking a fine line with my young daughter. I still had her, but I could tell we were at a crossroad. I couldn't let her give up on me. We had shared so many years together, with my needs and wants being a top priority, that I desperately needed to focus my time and attention on my growing child. I couldn't lose her. I could tell that if I continue use, came home from jail and got high, went back to jail, or failed to rebuild our lives, she would give up on me. She would turn to my mother and my brother for her care, love, and support. She would stop needing and relying on me—her mother. I could not lose my Laila. She was thirteen years old now, an age where changes are frequent and dramatic, unexpected and emotional. I needed to be there for her—to guide her, to support her, to comfort and encourage her and she approached her teenage years. It was my job and my privilege, my responsibility, to help her successfully learn and grow, to develop and experience life through adolescence. My selfish desires had to be put aside. Laila's well-being and future were more important. I could not have her give up on me. I could not lose her.

3. Jail: this is a huge deterrent for me because I find incarceration to be intolerable. I was able to discover spiritual change and personal transformation behind the walls, but I will never downplay the important role physical freedom plays in one's overall well-being. Freedom is certainly one of our basic needs as human beings and for me, it has always been at the top. We are given the ability to choose and to decide and to act on our own free will and this luxury determines the whos and whens and wheres of my life. I value freedom more than most of the other virtues and while in jail, freedom is restricted. I longed to touch grass, to sit on a sandy beach, to walk in the park with my mom and Laila, to buy a bottle of water, to send a text message, to hug my child and play with my nephews. These small every day occur-

rences are often taken for granted, but when they are taken away, the realization comes that they are precious.

Repeatedly reminding myself of these main three objections to using: the relationship with my mom, the responsibility I had to Laila, and the confinement of jail, kept me focused on what is truly important (recovery) and what I have to do to maintain those things I value the most (stay clean).

Another hurdle to overcome in early recovery was the persistent and vivid drug dreams. I often woke up remembering every detail involved in the dream: the getting of the drugs, the rituals of preparing the drugs, and finally, the using of the drugs. The dreams were terrible and would sometimes occur so often that I dreaded falling asleep. After the fourth night in a row of drug dreams, I finally mentioned it to Bruce during my drug and alcohol group. He was furious at me! How could I have let this go on, night after night, for so long, without mentioning it? I was in dangerous territory. The dreams would also come back to me throughout the day, as a spontaneous image flashing across my mind. They troubled me greatly—stressing me out, increasing cravings, and creating anxiety. I had simply been hoping they would end. Meanwhile, I found myself to be off centered, irritable, unfocused, and at times bordering on being rude. The disease had me. I thought I would be okay, I thought I'd get through it just fine, I figured it would pass. Bruce reminded me of how vital it is to share everything that is related to my addiction. Anything going on that takes me back to the old life needs to be promptly addressed and discussed. That includes the unpredictable, uncontrollable occurrence of drug dreams.

I came to recognize—very clearly—what my triggers were. Granted, people places and things need to be avoided. But I used everywhere, while doing everything—the whole world, the entire town—life itself—was a trigger! I had to learn about avoidable and unavoidable triggers. I will never again in my life need to be on the corners where I used to cop drugs. I can foresee no reason for ever having to step foot there again—or at least for today. That is an avoidable trigger. Veins are a huge trigger, so I do not inspect my body or yours, staring at the veins where I used to or could inject. Even rubbing lotion on my body after a shower triggered me.

Needles. Probably my top number one trigger. To recall a syringe filling up with blood and then pressing the plunger filled with cocaine into my veins makes me unmanageable and insane. My stomach tightens, my hands sweat, and my body shakes. That's a trigger to avoid. I have not yet had to have blood drawn at a doctor's office or hospital, but I am aware that I will need proper support and preparation when and if it becomes necessary for me to do so. They could not find an accessible vein when I came into the jail, so I escaped the experience of having blood drawn that time. For whatever reason, I am horribly obsessed with shooting up. That is my number one avoidable trigger. I don't glamorize it, dwell on it, or ponder the thought longer than the instant I recognize it's there. If anything will ever lead me back to using, it is needles. I know this about myself and I protect myself from harm's way. This is why knowing my personal triggers was so important. If I can know what it is that I'm facing, then I know what I'm up against. This way I can best equip myself to handle the triggering situation appropriately.

I also cannot dwell on experiences or people related to my using. This puts my thinking in relapse mode and steers me away from recovery. The lure of memories, flashbacks, and thoughts about life in active addiction, spontaneously at times, scare me and remind me to pray and turn my attention to recovery. Obviously sitting in the company of people who are sharing drug stories subjects me to euphoric recall, weakens my focus and renders me vulnerable to attack. I need to remain constantly vigilant about protecting my overall well-being. When recovery and freedom and life are most important to me, I will work diligently to ensure continued growth so that God's presence stays awake within me.

There are certain things that I had to stop doing or that I had to let go of. I could no longer speak harmfully or hurtfully. I was never a big one for cursing, but in addiction, there is a different protocol for language. Now I could feel the negative affect on me from the harmful words. I would walk my daily routine around the block and would hear cursing from every mouth I passed. I would literally cringe as I went by, feeling like a sharp pin prick had gone into my energy field. Ouch. I began to feel the effects of people's words—and my own words. And I began to choose carefully and cautiously what came out of my mouth. The negative and vicious words so common in jail hurt me and my spirit. Actually, literally hurt. I could not tolerate to listen to or hear the filth. It inflicted painful dissonance in my infinite spirit. One time I actually eavesdropped on two conversations for an entire hour while sitting in the day room. I told myself it was just like watching an immoral sitcom, so I justified my continued listening. The effects were enlightening—it was not the same as a bad TV show—it was worse, much worse. I had a pounding intense headache for three hours until I could meditate and mentally clear myself of the negativity. Words are profoundly powerful.

About four months into my stay in jail, Bruce mentioned in group about the harmful effects of stimulant drugs—including caffeine. I had relatively been okay with my intake of caffeine, but now Bruce made me think twice. I did see tolerance developing, a classic sign of addiction. Where once I only needed one cup, I now was having two sometimes three cups of coffee a day. In the beginning, one scoop of instant coffee and two scoops of creamer was enough. Then it progressed to two scoops of coffee and three to four scoops of creamer. In addition, consequences were beginning to appear, another addiction detector. I couldn't sleep at night or I slept restlessly at best. If I had any coffee after lunch, I would be awake half the night. I felt jittery and I had overwhelming racing thoughts. I had to be honest with myself—caffeine was a problem. I prayed, gave away the rest of my coffee, and decided to quit. I knew I had the strength from God to persevere through any withdrawal effects and patiently work through the lethargy until my brain once again learned to create its own endorphins naturally. And I survived. I had headaches and felt fatigued for a few days, but it all passed. I remember a few girls asked me for coffee that week and I had said that I gave it up. Their reactions were hilarious. The one girl was shocked, almost stunned. She asked me horrified, "Why?" The other girl said, "Completely? Oh my God, I would never do that." I laughed inside, realizing that we were both playing the game of life but we were on entirely different playing fields.

Goals

So here I was, incarcerated and at the beginning of the rest of my life. I barely had anything left: a storage unit full of belongings, a cell phone, and a driver's license being held at the police station, a closet full of clothing at my mother's house, and a precious thirteen-year-old child waiting for me. On the outside, it would appear that I nothing. Very, very little. Yet within me, there was a tender soft, gentle spirit filled with the goodness and grace of God. I had grown light-years beyond the woman who had entered that jail. So as to never reactivate that vicious monster of an addiction again, I needed to set my sights on positive outcomes for the future. I stood at a turning point, possibly for the first time ever, where I could clearly and honestly evaluate my inner desires—the imprints written onto my heart by God. I set out to discover who I was in God's eyes.

Having worked through the steps again, doing a fifth step with a gracious AA member, I no longer felt the enormity of guilt and self-hatred that was previously with me constantly. Yes, I sat in jail and on a daily basis, was visually reminded of my past wrongs. But the pain and damage of the past did not hold me hostage. Like a craving, guilt feelings arose at the thought of old behaviors. In fact the spiritual experience had so cleansed me that looking back at any moment of my previous life—the entire thirty years—made me cringe with regret. I saw clearly how I could have done and been so much better, more attentive and aware. My entire previous existence had been plagued by a dark selfishness, where even the good times were shrouded in distraction and lack of intimacy. I had missed out on so much, I had lost so much time and connection. I truly did not "know" a single person in my life. Not my mother, my own daughter, or my siblings. I could ramble off mere superficial qualities like occupations and memories, but I could truly not tell you about the heart of a single other person. My selfishness had always come first, robbing me of this privilege—to truly know and understand another person. What makes them hurt, angry, sad, or joyful? What do they think of themselves? What is their view, perspective, and understanding of the world? What do they dream about doing? Who do they long to become? What are their talents and natural abilities? What are their personal God-given gifts?

This insight made me profoundly sad. I had been so concerned with myself, that others did not matter. Now I was in jail and separated from those I desperately wanted to be with. I had a deep desire to understand others, to be there, to listen to them, to hear them. Most importantly, I wanted to start with Laila.

It may seem horrendous that a mother would not know her own daughter and this was a painful reality I was forced to face. I had always had high standards for myself as a mother, yet I was never able to be the mother I knew I could be because addictions always distracted me from my intentions and thwarted my ambitions. By not taking the time to relate to and understand Laila as a unique and individual person, I had never taught her how to get to know herself. Important questions were missed, such as: Who are you? What do you like, need, desire, and dream? What are the things you resent, or fear, or worry about? What brings you the greatest joy?

I had left her alone to answer these questions on her own in the materialistic world—the media induced, electronic age, which can quickly grab kids away from developing a personal choice. They like what's popular and what brings success. They do what the society tells them to do. I was unavailable to help Laila form a solid foundational sense of self, thereby leaving her vulnerable to be swept away by the influence of others. Now, clean and clear-minded, I longed to know my daughter and to teach her the value of knowing and deciding for herself. Who she was and what she wanted. It takes time, love, and dedicated attention to know another human being well enough to specifically be able to guide them onto the most fulfilling path. I felt that it was my responsibility as a mother—to take the time to understand Laila, in order to bring about her talents, strengthen her skills, and encourage her dreams. But before I could assist Laila in creating a great life for herself, I had to first teach her how to know herself.

This task did not always come easy for me in personal application. In fact, I never knew who I was or where I fit in or in what group I belonged to. I never purposefully set out to discover my strengths and weaknesses. I hated the word limitations. If I had a not-so-nice quality, I had always thought that there was something inherently morally wrong with me. With this believe, I was afraid to find out who I was. I avoided having to spend any time at all with myself because it was horrible and uncomfortable.

All that changed when I realized "whose" I was—I belong to God and I was His child. I saw for the first time ever the massive greatness of the spirit—embodied in this tiny human body. What a reversal in thinking. I had previously sought to punish myself for the secret horrible person I knew I was inside. Yet with God's purification and forgiveness, His spiritual cleansing showed me what an awesome responsibility I have. I reflect God's greatness—that is my job, my purpose, my entire goal. My be-all and end-all. I have a responsibility as God's child to express God's magnificence, which is a part of me through the Spirit. Wow! I not only can or should—but I must—let great things happen to me, for me, and through me! What a gift!

By discovering whose I was, I realized who I was. Both answers were simple: I am God's child. With that came the honor of bearing His glory. I understood that I had an obligation to manifest greatness in order to exhibit God's greatness. I also understood that my default nature was always going to be addiction. In order to protect and maintain my spiritual being, I needed to remain constantly vigilant—choosing goodness and grace over and over and over again. If I stray too far away from being centered in Christ, I revert back to my old tendencies—which bring pain, shame, remorse, and regret. I don't like being in my old nature today—I know too well the bliss and freedom of keeping my home close to God. But I do and will continue to fall back because this journey is a continuous process of growth, maturation, and sanctification. To continue in my daily pursuit of glorifying God, I need to always remember that I reflect my source in the way I live. A person's priorities and commitment are shown in the choices they make. In all I think and feel and say and do—in all that I am—I show the world my image of God. Today that image radiates and glows.

I began to discover secret passions; hidden dreams began to unlock inside the doors of my heart. I started to understand that God's imprints were deep within me, placed there purposefully by the hand of my Creator. I started to see gifts, fruits, and blessings of the Spirit becoming my natural responses.

I wanted to learn more about my personal gifts and talents so I began to consider what it is that I loved. There are things in life that enthrall me so much that I literally feel alive, enkindled with the power of love. I could spend forever in the experience without losing energy or being drained because when I am truly overtaken by God's spirit, expressing it and sharing it only adds fuel to the energy of the fire. It's those things I enjoy doing so much, that payment seems ludicrous. When the activity ends, I am more joyful and radiant and inspired then when I started. Maybe I am now just coming to catch up with things the rest of the world has always known. Follow my dreams. Listen to my heart. Trust my intuition. Let my conscience be my guide. That still, quiet voice grows louder as I pay attention to it more. Practice leads to change.

By walking closely in faith, a remarkable transformation occurred: God's will became my own true will for myself. I have come to know and desire the joy that comes from obedience—knowing and loving and serving and trusting my life into the hands of God. For me, these have been the keys to surrender and the basis for peace.

- Obeying: saying yes to God; accepting guidance and discipline and correction; submission to God's will.

- Knowing: seeing God in all situations; understanding His mysterious incomprehensible divinity; recognizing God in beauty and love and nature.
- Trusting: "Unzippering" myself before the Lord—completely open and exposed; giving my all to God—everything that I am.
- Serving: being an example of God's greatness; living as an ambassador for Christ; carrying God's message.
- Loving: glorifying God through every action; praising God with every thought; honoring God in every moment.

The ability to see God in everything is a breakthrough in perspective that forever changes the way a person relates to the world. When I know God's fingerprints are on every situation of my life, I no longer have struggles or problems. Life becomes an opportunity to discover and express God's greatness.

Looking at the world through that awareness, life becomes an exciting adventure lived in blessed assurance and confident expectation, awaiting with joyous curiosity the wonders God will create. In every moment, my only job is to let God shine. I am filled with overflowing gratitude at the privilege of being invested with such an honor. God, the Most High, wants to work with me! All I have to do is be an open and receptive vehicle and give God praise for the miracles that He creates through me. Who knew? Be a drug-addicted selfish criminal or a messenger of God's miracles?

God's joy fulfills in such great abundance that cocaine feels like a weak smile on a sorrowful face. I longed for purpose and meaning and fulfillment. Through God, in recovery, I found something extraordinary—something I didn't know existed—the light of God within me. When my being glows bright, illuminated with the Spirit, there is no need for anything. In those moments, I am already all there is. Nothing to be found or fixed or cured or changed or improved upon. Just me, radiating God. The ability to access that state of unlimitedness is everything I have ever wanted. This entryway has been the miracle of incarceration. I was once lost, broken, and hopeless—God made the impossible possible for me. Confined by metal doors and concrete walls, I discovered freedom.

There were only two small mirrors in jail and I rarely looked into either. In fact I didn't go near them for five months and when I did, I stood speechless at what I saw. As a child, I remember seeing a girl with bright blue eyes, soft complexion, long thick eyelashes and a pretty smile. Prior to incarceration, I remember seeing a face with sad eyes, hiding lies and inner turmoil. When I looked into the mirror that day in jail, my image shocked me. Who was this? I saw a peaceful radiance, a brilliant soul, and a soft warm spirit. I had lived for so long in the shadow of man's fallen nature, in the dark blackness of addiction. With new eyes, I was unrecognizable, even to myself. I was seeing the image of God. I was looking at my reflection in God's mirror out of the lenses of my own eyes.

ABOUT THE AUTHOR

Sara Colvin is a woman in recovery from drug and alcohol addiction. She lays out her personal experience in a captivating and heartfelt fashion. She has experienced the underworld of addiction as well as the beautiful life which recovery will bring.

Those still battling with active addiction will relate to her pain and suffering, while finding comfort in her recovery process. Those who have already found their way to a place of peace and restoration will identify with the transformation of her life after she puts the drugs down.

Overall, anyone reading Ms. Colvin's story is sure to be impacted by the tragedy and brutality characterized by a lifestyle of drugs and alcohol. Additionally, every reader will walk away with a renewed sense of hope and inspiration that is clearly outlined in the story of a soul rebuilt.

Ms. Colvin resides in the suburbs of Philadelphia. She passionately helps others find their way into the recovery community.